The Laws of Yahweh

A Handbook of Biblical Law

The Laws of Yahweh

A Handbook of Biblical Law

by

William J. Doorly

PAULIST PRESS
New York / Mahwah, N.J.

Book design by Theresa M. Sparacio

Cover design by Valerie Petro

Library of Congress Cataloging-in-Publication Data

Doorly, William J., 1931–
    The laws of Yahweh : a handbook of biblical law / by William J. Doorly.
      p. cm.
    Includes bibliographical references and index.
    ISBN 0-8091-4037-3
    1. Jewish law—Sources. I. Title.

    BM520.65 .D66 2002
    221.6′7—dc21

                                   2001058806

Published by Paulist Press
997 Macarthur Boulevard
Mahwah, New Jersey 07430

www.paulistpress.com

Printed and bound in the
United States of America

Contents

Charts

Acknowledgments

That this book is in your hands is in great measure the result of encouragement and technical assistance provided for me when I participated in an in-depth Bible study series during the fall of 2000.

I started this book as early as January 1999. In June of that year I had a heart attack and was hospitalized three times in less than a month. I tried to continue this biblical law project, in which I had great interest, for the next year but found that concentration and energy were in low supply.

In the fall of 2000 I participated in a Bible study program at the Thomas Paine Unitarian Universalist Fellowship of Eagleville, Pennsylvania. One of the topics we investigated was "The Laws of the Torah." I mentioned that I had doubts about my ability to continue with this handbook, but some of the members of the study group would not accept this. Encouragement to continue came in the form of software, hardware, labor support, and technical assistance. I must acknowledge my thanks to a core group consisting of Don Carter, Curt Stauffer, Jacque Hurley, and Carol Klekotka. Although not a member of the group, Chris Eldridge also provided me with an opportunity to update my word processing skills during 2001.

Sometimes what we need in life are friends who won't take no for an answer. I continue to be indebted to the editorial staff of the Paulist Press whose collective patience reminds me of 1 Corinthians 13:4:

Love is patient.

1

The Religion of Judah
Becomes Preoccupied with Law

It is quite likely that the first time a written law code occupied a central place in the royal religion of Judah was during the reign of Josiah (640–609 B.C.E.) when the *seper hattorah* (book of the law) was discovered in the temple. It is essential to note that the reign of Josiah came to a tragic end only twenty-three years before the end of Judah as an independent political entity. In 586 the neo-Babylonians, whom we know to have been Chaldeans, destroyed the city of Jerusalem, demolished and burned the temple of Solomon, and carried away many of the elite of Jerusalem into Babylonian captivity.

The account of Josiah's reign in its final, canonical form is well crafted, containing many segments. When we break down its elements we realize that much detail is included in only two chapters (2 Kgs 22—23).

While we are aware of several layers of authorship in the account of Josiah's reign, we do not believe that this understanding negates the historical basis for the reformation activity of Josiah. The reformation stressed a perception of Yahweh who was preoccupied with the keeping of a law. This law was based on a Deuteronomic theology, and the book of the law was at least a portion of the Deuteronomic Law Code (Deut 12–26).

There are several clues to inform us that the canonical account of Josiah's reform contains more than one layer of authorship. The clue that concerns us here is the appearance of two different names for the scroll of law that Josiah read to the people. In 2 Kings 22:8 and 22:11 the discovered scroll is called *the book of the law:*

> The High priest Hilkiah said to Shaphan the secretary, "I have found the book of the law in the house of the LORD."…When the king heard the words of the book of the law, he tore his clothes.

1

Later, in the account of Josiah reading to the people, the name of the scroll is changed to *the book of the covenant:*

> The king went up to the house of the LORD, and with him went all the people of Judah....He read in their hearing all the words of the book of the covenant. (2 Kgs 23:2)

The Production of Scrolls in Judah

Whatever role the collections of laws played in ancient Israel, a new age began for the central place the scrolls would play in the official religion of Judah during the reign of Josiah. The fascinating narrative account of the discovery of the book of the law (2 Kgs 22—23) and the subsequent reading of this scroll to

> all the inhabitants of Jerusalem, the priests, the prophets, and all the people, both small and great (2 Kgs 23:2–3)

BIBLICAL EXAMPLES OF PUBLIC READING/ RECITATION OF LAW[1]

CHART 1a

HISTORICAL

1. Josiah in Jerusalem at the temple	*2 Kgs 23:1–3*
2. Ezra in square before the Water Gate	*Neh 8*

NON-HISTORICAL PROJECTIONS INTO ISRAEL'S PAST

3. Moses in the wilderness, near Sinai	*Exod 34:32–33*
4. Moses, east of the Jordan River	*Deut 5:24–28*
5. Joshua between Mounts Ebal and Gerazim	*Josh 8:30–35*

---

was part of an ambitious program to educate the people of Judah in accordance with the goals of a marginal Levitical priesthood whose ancestry can be traced to the Shechem area in the former northern nation-state of Israel.[2] Modern scholars have called this marginal group of priests and scribes the Deuteronomic circle. The source of this name is obviously based on the name later given to the book that appears as a prologue to the history of Israel/Judah that these Levitical priests produced. *Deuteronomy* was a word these priests never heard or used. The individual books of their history would later be named Joshua, Judges, Samuel, and Kings.

The goal of this circle was to centralize and standardize an official, Yahweh-only cult in Judah while at the same time creating a strong nationalistic spirit among the fragmented people of Judah. During the reign of Josiah, Assyria, the great military and political power from Mesopotamia, which had dominated, terrorized, and exploited the small nations of the ancient Near East for three centuries (900–600), was collapsing under its own weight, and its demise was in sight. The decline of Assyria was seen by Judah as a magnificent opportunity to create a new golden age that would include the annexation of Samerina, the former territory of the nation-state Israel that once was part of the kingdom of David and Solomon. The Deuteronomic circle had great vision. To reach its goals of unification in Judah and annexation of the north the circle saw a pressing need for vast public education that included the use of authorized scrolls containing Israel's history and Israel's authorized laws. Because the common people of Judah/Israel did not have the ability to read, and the few who did had little access to writings, scroll production for the purpose of public readings came into its own late in the seventh century. We maintain that the influential circle of Levitical priests which traced its ancestry to Shechem was the leader in recognizing the value of scroll production for didactic purposes. We will comment below on how the Aaronid priests of the temple later adopted scroll production on their own, following the lead of the Levites.

The Deuteronomic History

Scholars have discovered that an early, optimistic version of the Deuteronomic History appeared during the reign of Josiah. In this Josianic version of the Deuteronomic History, Joshua the person was presented as an ancient version of Josiah, and Josiah a modern version of Joshua. In many vital ways these two leaders mirrored each other.[3] For our purposes in this handbook it is important to note that both Joshua and Josiah read from the book of the law *(seper hattorah)* to the people, and that not one other leader in Deuteronomic History—military, royal, or priestly—ever read from this collection of law. In the Deuteronomic History we are asked to believe that the book of the law was lost for centuries, but that it had originated from the mouth of Yahweh, entrusted to Moses.

The Deuteronomic perception of Yahweh presented in the Deuteronomic History included an emphasis on the *learning and observance of the law*. Yahweh was perceived of as a God obsessed with the keeping of laws. While the intended use of scroll production for educational purposes originated with the Levitical priests whom scholars have called the Deuteronomic circle, it is true that the official priests of the Jerusalem temple (sometimes called Aaronid or Zadokite) also produced scrolls. What was the relationship between the royal priests (Aaronid) and the marginal priests of the Deuteronomic circle (Levites)?[4] We can only speculate. If the reform program of the Deuteronomic circle was historical, including the role played by Josiah, it is reasonable to assume that the Josianic reformation could not have been attempted without the cooperation of the Aaronid priests. In the early phases of the Josianic reform it may be reasonable to assume that some form of alliance existed between the Levites and Aaronids. Although the Aaronids may have been wary of the efforts of the Shechemite Levites, they were impressed by their zeal for Yahweh. In the early stage of the Josianic reformation, the Deuteronomic circle was not seen as a threat to the royal priests. Both priesthoods would have believed that the centralization and standardization of the worship of Yahweh in Jerusalem as set forth in the Deuteronomic Law Code (Deuteronomy 12) would have been of great benefit to the state of Judah in particular and the people in general.

The Death of Josiah

In 609 B.C.E. Josiah was tragically killed at Megiddo, where he had gone to interrupt the eastern march of the Egyptian army toward Assyria under the leadership of Pharaoh Neco. Following the untimely death of Josiah incongruities between the theology of the two priesthoods (Shechemite and Aaronid) resurfaced and became more evident, and cooperative effort came to a halt. But the Deuteronomic circle had produced an early version of the magnificent scrolls that would later become the core of the Hebrew Bible, and the functionality of scroll use for public education was not lost on the priests of the royal temple. The Aaronids, influenced by the Deuteronomists, would later begin to include law as a central part of their educational program.

But the scrolls produced by the Aaronides had a different emphasis. The laws with which they would start their collection (the Priestly Code) were originally laws found in priestly manuals concerning temple procedures, offerings, vestments, furniture, sacrifices, architecture of the temple, and so forth. In a later collection a concept of *holiness*—ritual cleanliness—would be set forth that would become a trademark of the Tetrateuchal source which scholars would later designate by the letter P. The other documentary sources of the Tetrateuch, J, E, and D,[5] appear now in the canonical Bible as the result of a brilliant redactional effort by the royal Aaronid priests in Babylonian captivity.

The Law Collections of the Aaronids

Although the Aaronids started their two law collections (the Holiness Code and the Priestly Code) by using the regulations of priestly manuals, they would follow the lead of the Shechemite Levites (the Deuteronomic circle) by adding civil laws and laws concerning secular morality. Another way in which the Aaronids would follow the lead of the Deuteronomic circle was in supplying a narrative setting for the source and presentation of law. The Deuteronomists had provided a historical environment for their law collection that involved Moses, Joshua, and the Israelite nation on the verge of entering Canaan.[6] Moses was said to pass the book of the law to Joshua, who carried it across the Jordan into the land promised to the children of Jacob (Israel). The Aaronids decided to select an earlier historical period, the period spent in the wilderness, for the origin of their law collections. Israel was said to have received her laws at Sinai. Following the lead of the Deuteronomists, Moses appeared at the center of their story.

The Four Collections of Law

The canonical version of the Hebrew Bible contains four collections of law (see Chart 1b). All four are found recorded in the Pentateuch and are associated historically with the location of a great theophany at Mount Sinai. In Deuteronomy, however, the place of theophany is referred to as Horeb.[8]

The plan of this handbook is first to examine each collection of law separately in this order: the Book of the Covenant (Exod 21—23), the Deuteronomic Law Code (Deut 12—26), the Holiness Code (Lev 17—26), and the Priestly Code (spread throughout Exodus, Leviticus, and Numbers). We will then look at the decalogues of the Torah, followed by an attempt to make sense out of those passages that refer to the administration of justice in ancient Israel. We will continue by comparing the laws of biblical Israel with other law collections of the ancient Near East. We will conclude with an essay on the blending of law and narrative in the Pentateuch during the captivity period.

A widely known Talmudic tradition states that there are 613 laws in the Torah, the first five books of the Hebrew Bible. Negative laws or prohibitions number 365 and positive laws 248. Talmudic tradition did not identify the 613 laws, but later medieval scholars listed them in several ways. We will discuss these laws in chapter 6, "The Rabbinical Tradition of 613 Laws."

At the conclusion of each chapter dealing with the four law collections (chapters 2 through 5) we will print an index of the laws discussed. Part II of this book contains an index of all of the laws of the Pentateuch.

COLLECTIONS AND SUMMARIES OF THE LAW FOUND IN THE HEBREW BIBLE

CHART 1b

1. There are four collections of law in the Hebrew Bible. All four are found in the Pentateuch.

2. These four collections are:

   The Book of the Covenant (Exod 20:22—23:19)
   The Deuteronomic Code (Deut 12—26)
   The Holiness Code (Lev 17—26)
   The Priestly Code (Scattered throughout Exodus, Leviticus, and Numbers)

3. Decalogues of the law include the Ethical Decalogue, Exodus 20:1–17 and Deuteronomy 5:6–21, and the Ritual Decalogue, Exodus 34:12–26.

4. All the collections of the law and the decalogues are said to come to a united Israel from Yahweh through Moses.

5. Both the collections and decalogues contain a combination of sacred (cultic) and secular (social) laws.

6. All four collections in their canonical forms are considered to have signs of literary growth and often include inserted subsections, editorial comments, and interpretative remarks.

7. The narrative context of the four collections involves a mountain of God, usually called Sinai. In Deuteronomy the mountain is called Horeb.[8]

2

The Covenant Code
Exodus 20:22—23:19

The so-called Book of the Covenant, which we will refer to as the Covenant Code, is a collection of laws found in Exodus 20—23.[1] According to our count, there are fifty-two laws here.[2] The first thing that should suggest itself to our minds is that if there are approximately fifty-two laws, the Covenant Code cannot be a complete law code. There are too few laws, and most areas of life are not touched. This is true of all four of the collections of laws in the Pentateuch. We do not have anything that resembles a complete law code for all Israel or even an identifiable area of Israel.[3]

Laws from Different Periods

Although the Covenant Code may contain some of the oldest laws in the Hebrew Bible, we will not make the mistake of calling this collection the oldest of Israel's law codes. The reason for this is that in this collection, as with the other collections we will be examining, new and old may stand side by side, and each individual law, and cluster of laws within the larger collections as we have received them, may have originated in different locations at different times in Israel's history. One thing that scholars agree on is that the Covenant Code is the result of complex editorial development. Many of the laws are laws of a settled agricultural community, but that observation in itself cannot date the laws. Israel was a settled agricultural community for centuries, indeed for most of her existence. Laws concerning resident aliens (Exod 22:21; 23:9) may have originated during the period following the destruction of the northern kingdom when refugees from Israel began to surface in Judah in sizeable numbers.

You shall not oppress a resident alien; you know the heart of an alien,
for you were aliens in the land of Egypt. (Exod 23:9)

The laws concerning a Hebrew debt slave would not have developed in the premonarchical period. It is generally agreed that debt slavery may have been a social problem in the eighth century but may also have been a reality anywhere from the ninth century to the end of the seventh century.

Also, some scholars have associated this collection with the reformation of Hezekiah, who reigned in the closing decades of the eighth century, but the cultic laws opening this code (Exod 20:23–26) do not support destruction of local altars or centralization of Yahweh worship. There is a law that forbids invoking the name of a god other than Yahweh (Exod 23:13), but this law is part of the cultic epilogue. There is no law requiring the destruction of high places, the crushing of pillars, or the cutting down of sacred poles such as we find in the Ritual Decalogue (Exod 34) and the Deuteronomic Code (Deut 12—26). If the reformation of Hezekiah was historical, the cultic introduction would not have supported his activity.

He [Hezekiah] removed the high places, broke down the pillars and cut down the sacred pole. (2 Kgs 18:4)[4]

The Name *Book of the Covenant*

The popular name of this ancient law collection is unfortunate, because the word *covenant (berit)*[5] is a theologically loaded word. Centuries after the Sinai period in which the Book of the Covenant/Covenant Code is located, the word *covenant* came to be associated with an elaborate metaphor built on a form of the vassal treaty that superpowers of the ancient Near East used to establish the role which small, subservient nation-states (Syria, Israel, Judah, Philistia, Edom, and Moab) would play in the political scheme of international politics. In the vassal relationship the small nation-states would be allowed to maintain some independence and self-rule (which was to the advantage of the superpower) while acknowledging the superiority of the nation imposing the vassal treaty and sending to the king of the conquering nation tribute on a regular basis, including silver, gold, produce, supplies, skilled persons, laborers, and so forth. The relationship established between the two political entities was a cross between a master/servant relationship and parent/child relationship. By itself, the Covenant Code *has nothing to do with the vassal treaty form*, and the traditional name found in Exodus 24:7 is therefore misleading.[6]

The Book of Exodus

Modern scholars recognize that the Covenant Code was not originally part of the Sinai tradition.[7] To clarify this we must say a few things about the book of Exodus. Exodus in its canonical form was assembled during the Babylonian exile[8] under the supervision of former temple priests, known as Aaronid priests, and their descendants in captivity. More than a century and a half earlier, Israel, the northern kingdom, had ceased to exist, having been destroyed by the Assyrians (Shalmanesar V and Sargon II) in 722 B.C.E. Judah, the southern kingdom where Jerusalem was located, although it survived for more than a century longer than Israel, was finally destroyed by the neo-Babylonians in several stages from 597 to 586 B.C.E.

For the Aaronid priests (probably the former priests of the Jerusalem temple) the exile became a time of creative theological reorganization, and we know that the importance of the exodus tradition grew tremendously, playing a key role in the rethinking and re-creating of Israel's past. In captivity the name Egypt became a code word for Babylon.

We would like to know more about the role and understanding of the exodus tradition in Jerusalem during the period following the destruction of the northern kingdom of Israel (722) and before the final destruction of Jerusalem (586). This is a fascinating area of study, and while it is not our goal to review the myriad possibilities, we can assume that the exodus tradition played a lesser role in pre-exilic, monarchic Jerusalem, having nothing like the centrality it would assume during the exile.[9]

In putting together the scroll of Exodus, the Aaronid priests used several ancient sources, the chief of which may have been the J (Jahweh or J[Y]ahwist) source and the E (Elohim or Elohist) source. The exilic priests who produced the new scroll of Exodus are referred to by scholars by the letter P (for Priestly). P added their own material and made editorial decisions in accordance with their own guidelines and goals concerning how the sources J and E would be used, and how they would be sectioned and fitted together within the P structure.[10]

The major themes of Exodus include the deliverance of a population of slave laborers from Egypt (all of whom were children of Jacob, even though aliens seem to be part of the wilderness mix), guidance through the wilderness, and a theophany at Sinai. Included in the exilic version of the Sinai tradition is the giving of written laws in several forms. These laws include the Ten Commandments (Exod 20:1–21), the Covenant Code (Exod 20:22—23:19), a collection of priestly laws associated with the tabernacle (Exod 25—31), and a set of ritual commandments (34:17–26) sometimes contrasted with the Ethical Decalogue.

The Covenant Code in its present location may be part of a covenant-making narrative framework (sometimes called a covenant renewal ceremony/ritual) that begins in Exodus 19 and continues through Exodus 24. The four parts of the covenant narrative are (1) Covenant proposal, (2) Anticipatory acceptance, (3) Stipulations (the Covenant Code), and (4) Ratification.

In Exodus 19 God (the divine ruler, suzerain) proposes a covenant relationship between himself and Israel (the vassal). God tells Moses what to say to the people:

> You have seen what I did to the Egyptians and how I bore you on eagles' wings and brought you to myself. Now therefore, if you obey my voice and keep my covenant, you shall be my treasured possession out of all the peoples. (Exod 19:4–5)

Moses sets the words of God before the people, and the people respond positively.

> Everything that the LORD has spoken we will do. (Exod 19:8)

Of course the heart of a vassal treaty is the body of stipulations (laws) that the vassal must understand and agree to accept from the supreme ruler. In Exodus 20 through 23 we have two sets of laws representing the vassal treaty stipulations, the result of a complex editorial growth of the canonical book, the Ethical Decalogue (Exod 20:1–17), followed by the Covenant Code (Exod 20:22—23:19).[11]

In Exodus 24 we are told that Moses wrote down the laws of the Lord and read them to the people.

> Then he [Moses] took the book of the covenant, and read it in the hearing of the people; and they said All that the LORD has spoken we will do, and we will be obedient. (Exod 24:7)

The ratification of the covenant was completed when seventy elders of the people ate and drank in the presence of the God of Israel on the mountain (Exod 24:9–11). We will discuss the Ethical Decalogue in chapter 7, "The Decalogues of the Torah."

The Origin of the Covenant Code

Our contention is that the earliest form of the Covenant Code had its origin in the territory of the northern tribes long after the supposed Sinai/wilderness period and was placed in its canonical location as a result of a priestly decision.[12] It is not possible to establish a firm date for several reasons:

(a) The collection comprises several sections and these sections (along with individual laws) did not originate at the same time. It is safer to understand that sections of the code originated in different places at different times. (b) While some scholars identify the agricultural laws concerning the responsibility for the goring ox (Exod 21:28–32), the open pit in the country (Exod 21:33), and laws regarding farm animals (Exod 22:9–14) as a sign of an early origin, possibly premonarchical, we must reply that all these agricultural laws were just as relevant for rural areas throughout the period of the northern kingdom as well as into late Judah (during the reign of Josiah, for example) as they would have been centuries earlier. In other words, they could have been reduced to writing at any time during Israel's existence. (c) Several commentaries cite the absence of references to the monarchy and the royal political structure as evidence of early origin.[13] This is a good example of an argument from silence. In the collections of law in the Pentateuch there is only one paragraph mentioning the monarchy (Deut 17:14–20).

It is frequently noted that the content of several laws predate Deuteronomy. For example, in Deuteronomy the law of the Hebrew slave is more refined and humanitarian than the earlier version in the Covenant Code.[14] Also, in the Covenant Code there is no limitation to one shrine chosen by Yahweh for his worship as is characteristic of Deuteronomy (Deut 12:4–13). We will discuss this further in chapter 3, "The Deuteronmic Law Code."

As to the location of the code's earliest formation, some scholars have stated that Shechem in the north is a safe guess.[15]

The Divisions of the Covenant Code

It is vital to understand that the collection under consideration is divided into two main parts (see Chart 2a): Part I (Exod 21:1—22:17), and Part II (Exod 22:18—23:9). In addition to these two parts or sections there is a cultic prologue concerning images of silver and gold, an altar of earth, an altar of hewn stones, and the steps to an altar (Exod 20:22–26).[16]

There is also a cultic epilogue concluding the Covenant Code (Exod 23:10–19) (see Charts 2a and 2b).

We will discuss the four parts of the Covenant Code in this order: Cultic Prologue, Part I, Part II, Cultic Epilogue. We believe that the prologue and epilogue were added to a previous listing of laws.

```
┌─────────────────────────────────────────────────────────────────┐
│                                                                   │
│              DIVISIONS OF THE COVENANT                             │
│              CODE IN ITS CANONICAL FORM                            │
│                                                                   │
│                      CHART 2a                                     │
│                                                                   │
├─────────────────────────────────────────────────────────────────┤
```

Prologue	Four cultic laws concerning images and altars. *Exod 20:22–26*
Part I	Twenty-two secular laws concerning property, bodily injury, and restitution. *Exod 21:1—22:17*
Part II	Twenty unconditional (apodictic) social and cultic laws often with exhortative language based on a divine demand for justice. *Exod 22:18—23:9*
Epilogue	Six cultic laws, including required participation in three annual festivals. *Exod 23:10–19*

The Prologue to the Covenant Code

Images of Silver and Gold, and an Altar of Earth

The prologue may have been added as an introduction to the body of the Covenant Code by scribes. It was the editorial practice of scribes to add new beginnings (even if the material was ancient) when updating or producing new copies of scrolls. Of course we do not know with certainty the origin of the prologue consisting of four cultic laws (Exod 20:22–26), but they are obviously primitive: (1) Images of Yahweh made of silver or gold are forbidden. (2) An altar for sacrifices should be made of earth. (3) If you make an altar of stones, it should not be of hewn stones. (4) You shall not use steps to reach your altar, because it may expose your nakedness.

A First-person Speaker Identifies Cultic Laws

The first thing we should notice about cultic laws is that there is a first-person speaker. The cultic laws found in the prologue and epilogue illustrate this. In the cultic prologue all four laws relate to *me* or to *my*:

> You shall not make gods of silver *alongside me*.... (20:23)
> You need make *for me* only an altar of earth.... (20:24)
> If you make *for me* an altar of stone.... (20:25)
> You shall not go up by steps *to my altar*.... (20:26)

In the cultic epilogue (Exod 23:12–19) there also are first-person references to the speaker:

> Be attentive to all that *I have said* to you.... (23:13)
> Three times in the year you shall hold a festival for me.... (23:14)
> No one shall appear *before me* empty-handed.... (23:15)
> You shall not offer the blood of *my sacrifice* with anything leavened, or let the fat of *my festival* remain until the morning.... (23:18)

Reading the cultic laws that now open the Covenant Code produces some interesting questions. Images of silver and gold are forbidden, but what does that say about images made of base materials? Most scholars assume that images were forbidden all over Israel from primitive times.

The requirement that altars be made of earth may refer to sun-dried mud bricks but is in conflict with the next law concerning the use of stones.

> If you make for me an altar of stone... (20:25)

The requirement of the use of unhewn stones for altars is one of the few laws mentioned specifically in the Deuteronomic History:

> Then Joshua built on Mount Ebal an altar to the LORD ..."an altar of unhewn stones, on which no iron tool has been used." (Josh 8:31)

The exhortative remark that follows the altar of earth requirement signifies that there will be altars at multiple sites:

> In *every place* where I cause my name to be remembered I will come to you and bless you. (Exod 20:24, emphasis added)

We notice that the speaker (God) refers to his name. Is this an early example of the *name theology,* a later trademark of the Deuteronomic circle?

The prohibition of altar steps raises further questions. Persons making the sacrifices on an altar with steps are not aware of the required priestly attire of the Aaronid priests as described in a section of priestly legislation now found in Exodus 28:42:

> You shall make for them [Aaronid priests] linen undergarments to cover their naked flesh; they shall reach from the hips to the thighs.[17]

But would the two or three steps up to a rural altar reveal someone's naked-ness? Altars with steps have been discovered at Lachish, Megiddo, and Bethshan.

The literary question is this. Could the prologue once have been attached to Part II, which contains apodictic (unconditional) laws, some of which are cult related and are often presented as the voice of a god, possibly Yahweh? It is possible that all of Part I consisting of casuistic laws was *inserted* after the prologue and before the apodictic laws of what we call Part II.

Some feel that the cultic laws of the prologue are more ancient than the laws found in the epilogue. The epilogue mentions the required three annual festivals (see Chart 2e). This requirement assumes widespread organization of the people that would not have existed in the first days of Israel's emergence in the highlands of Canaan. Also, the penultimate cultic law of the epilogue comes from a later period than the earthen altar law. The house of the LORD is mentioned:

> The choicest of the first fruits of your ground you shall bring into the *house of the LORD* your God. (Exod 23:19, emphasis added)

CULTIC LAWS IN THE PROLOGUE AND EPILOGUE OF THE COVENANT CODE

CHART 2b

Cultic Prologue: Exodus 20:22–26

- Images of gold and silver forbidden
- Only an altar of earth permitted
- Altars of hewn stones forbidden
- Altar steps that could expose nakedness forbidden

Cultic Epilogue: Exodus 23:10–19

- Observe a weekly sabbath.
- Do not invoke the names of other gods.
- All males shall participate in three annual festivals: feast of unleavened bread; feast of harvest; and festival of ingathering.
- Do not offer blood with anything leavened.
- Bring the choicest fruits to the house of your God.
- Boiling a kid in its mother's milk is forbidden.

This law assumes a central place of worship for an area and could refer to a temple building at a large cult site.

Part I of the Covenant Code[18]

Part I begins with two laws that have been called slave laws; continues with laws related to bodily injury and care of livestock and other property; and concludes with a law related to marriage. Most of the twenty-two laws in Part I (Exod 21:1—22:17) are casuistic laws. The German scholar Albrecht Alt popularized the definition of two types of biblical laws that have been called casuistic and apodictic. In the casuistic laws (case laws)[19] the word "when" is used frequently along with the word "if." For example:

> *When* individuals quarrel and one strikes the other with a stone or fist so that the injured party, though not dead, is confined to bed, but [*if* he] recovers and walks around outside with the help of a staff, then the assailant shall be free of liability, *except* to pay for the loss of time, and to arrange for full recovery. (Exod 21:18–19, emphasis added)

The last law of Part I, like the example given above, illustrates the *when* and *if* pattern, and also the subsequent wordiness of casuistic laws:

> *When* a man seduces a virgin who is not engaged to be married, and lies with her, he shall give the bride-price *[mohar]* for her and make her his wife. *But if* her father refuses to give her to him, he shall pay an amount equal to the bride-price for virgins. (Exod 22:16–17, emphasis added)

Notice the subtlety used by the author in distinguishing between the bride-price and an amount equal to the bride-price. Notice also that the woman has no part in the decision making. Her father and the man who seduced her make the decisions concerning her fate in this matter. In the law collections we will find many examples of the paternalistic nature of society in ancient Israel.

The So-Called Law of the Female Slave

An early law of Part I states that a father can sell his daughter as a slave (Exod 21:7). Because of the opening words of this law an editor placed this law immediately following the law of the Hebrew slave. But this law is a marriage law, not a slavery law. Take away the first sentence—When a man sells his daughter as a slave, she shall not go out as the male slaves do. (Exod 21:7)—and read the rest of the law and it becomes clear that this is an arranged marriage law, plain and simple. First of all, the daughter is not a Hebrew but an Israelite.

It is our contention that the Hebrews were a marginal subculture within Israel. Second, there is no time period for release, as in the Hebrew slave law. Third, note how the following words identify the law as a marriage law:

> If he takes another wife to himself, he shall not diminish the food, clothing, or marital rights of *the first wife.* (Exod 21:10, emphasis added)

Summary of Part I

So the first half of the Covenant Code, Exodus 21:1—22:17, is made up chiefly of casuistic laws, laws using the words "when" and "if." Characteristic of Part I is that the laws are not cultic laws, related to the rituals of religion,

---

LAWS (MOSTLY CASUISTIC) OF PART I
OF THE COVENANT CODE
(EXODUS 21:2—22:17)

CHART 2c

---

1. When you buy a Hebrew slave. (21:2–6)
2. When a man sells his daughter as a slave. (21:7–11)
3. Whoever strikes a man and kills him. (21:12–14)
4. Whoever strikes father or mother. (apodictic, 21:15)
5. Whoever kidnaps a person. (apodictic, 21:16)
6. Whoever curses father or mother. (apodictic, 21:17)
7. When men quarrel and one strikes the other. (21:18–19)
8. When a man strikes his slave. (21:20–21)
9. When a pregnant woman is injured. (21:22–25)
10. When a man strikes the eye of his slave. (21:26–27)
11. When an ox gores a human. (21:28–32)
12. If someone leaves a pit open. (21:33–34)
13. When an ox injures a neighbor's ox. (21:35–36)
14. When a man steals an ox or a sheep. (22:1–2)
15. When a thief is beaten to death. (22:2b)
16. When livestock feeds in another's field. (22:5)
17. When fire destroys a field. (22:6)
18. When money/goods are given for safekeeping. (22:7–8)
19. When there is disputed ownership. (22:9)
20. When livestock is given for safekeeping. (22:10–13)
21. When a man borrows from another. (22:14)
22. If a man seduces a virgin. (22:16–17)

but deal with the ongoing social interaction and economic affairs of a rural, agricultural (settled, rather than nomadic) people.[20]

If the only difference between the laws of Part I and the laws of Part II were the casuistic characteristics, we could surmise that they were grouped together by an editor. But there are other differences between Part I and Part II that suggest the origins of the two parts involve different community locations and different time periods.

These are the characteristics of Part I (Exod 21:1—22:17): (a) In the casuistic laws the Lord does not speak. As a matter of fact, no one speaks.[21] Later, as we will see in Part II of the Covenant Code, where laws appear in an apodictic form, many laws are supported by words of exhortation presumed to be the direct words of Yahweh. Yahweh is the speaker, or assumed to be the speaker. (b) Because of the *when* and *if* clauses, the casuistic laws are wordy. (c) These laws have the character of having grown as a result of real life situations. (d) The casuistic laws reached their stated form as a part of a legal tradition and do not claim to be a revelation from God. It is implied that casuistic laws are the *end result of customary usage.* (e) Even though casuistic laws are wordy, they do not contain the preachy, exhortative remarks we will encounter in support of apodictic laws.

While we have pointed out that the casuistic laws comprising Part I are not presented as the words of Yahweh or any other god or authority, the name of Yahweh does appear once in Part I. In a wordy casuistic law concerning the holding of an animal by a neighbor for safekeeping we read:

> When someone delivers to another a donkey, ox, sheep, or any other animal for safekeeping, and it dies or is injured or is carried off, without anyone seeing it, an oath before the LORD [Yahweh] shall decide between the two of them that the one has not laid hands on the property of the other. (Exod 22:10–13)

Although the name of Yahweh is mentioned in this law, there is no suggestion that Yahweh had any part in originating this law or its revelation. This role of Yahweh as an originator of law is absent. Making an oath before Yahweh to determine who was telling the truth when there were no witnesses does not inform us that Yahweh played the major role in the theological perceptions of the community where these casuistic laws originated. At one time in Israel's history it is possible that for this rural community Yahweh could be called upon to determine who was telling the truth, a player in an ordeal. Also, note that there is no indication as to how the final decision would be recognized by the community or parties involved.

*Are the Law Collections of the Bible Typical of All Law Codes
in Ancient Israel?*

As we noted earlier, the four collections of law found in the Pentateuch were the production of priests with theological agenda. It is frequently
stated that law codes of ancient Israel mixed secular and cultic laws. This
statement must be modified. At this time we do not have copies of Israelite
law collections apart from the Hebrew Bible. It is possible that there were
collections of laws from some locations in Israel that have not been preserved and that we have not uncovered which were completely secular.

Apart from the scrolls of the Bible, we don't have a copy of a law code
of Israel. It is possible that Part I of the Covenant Code is a portion of a completely secular law code. We do have law codes and fragments of law codes
from other nations of the ancient Near East.[22] These codes are almost
entirely secular, but as we will see in chapter 9, "The Laws of the Ancient
Near East," they do contain laws that mention the names of gods.

Part II of the Covenant Code

The first law of Part II is a good illustration of an apodictic law:[23]

You shall not permit a female sorcerer to live. (Exod 22:18)

There are no *ifs, whens,* or *buts* here. Here are other examples:

You shall not delay to make offerings from the fullness of your harvest
and from the outflow of your presses. (Exod 22:29)
You shall not spread a false report. (23:1)

Many of the laws of Part II are prohibitions, as are the two examples above.
An example of a positive law is, for example,

When you come upon your enemy's ox or a donkey going astray, you
shall bring it back. (23:4)

God As Speaker

There are twenty laws in Part II, and several can be said to be the
words of God. Some examples are:

If you do abuse them, when they cry out to me, I will surely heed their
cry. (22:23)

Do not kill the innocent and those in the right, for I will not acquit the
guilty. (23:7)

No one shall appear before me empty-handed. (23:15)

**LAWS OF PART II OF THE COVENANT CODE
(EXODUS 22:18—23:19)**

CHART 2d

---

1. Concerning female sorcerers. (22:18)
2. Whoever lies with an animal. (22:19)
3. Whoever sacrifices to another god. (22:20)
4. The resident alien. (22:21)
5. The widow or orphan. (22:21)
6. Lending money to the poor. (22:25)
7. A neighbor's cloak in pawn. (22:26)
8. Reviling God or cursing a leader. (22:28)
9. Delay in making offering of your fullness. (22:29)
10. The firstborn of your sons, oxen, and sheep. (22:29–30)
11. Meat mangled by beasts. (22:31)
12. A false report (or being a malicious witness). (23:1)
13. Being partial in a lawsuit decision. (23:2–3)
14. Seeing a donkey gone astray. (23:4)
15. Seeing a burdened donkey of one who hates you. (23:5)
16. Justice due to the poor in their lawsuits. (23:6)
17. Innocent verdicts for those in the right. (23:7)
18. Taking no bribe. (23:8)
19. Not oppressing a resident alien. (23:9)
20. A seventh year of rest for fields, vineyards, and orchards. (23:10)

Yahweh is never the speaker in Part I (Exod 21:1—22:17). Yahweh is identified by name several times in Part II including:

> Whoever sacrifices to any god, other than the LORD [Yahweh] alone, shall be devoted to destruction. (Exod 22:20)

Exhortative Amendments to Laws

Another characteristic of Part II consists of words of moral encouragement added to an apodictic law to enhance the law. In several places didactic words have been added to a law by a concerned scribe. Scholars also call these exhortative remarks motive clauses. Some have referred to laws that have these exhortative remarks as the law preached. For example, the law concerning the receiving of your neighbor's cloak for security requires that the cloak be returned before the sun goes down. Then these explanatory words have been added:

> It may be your neighbor's only clothing to use as cover; in what else shall that person sleep? (Exod 22:27)

A law that forbids the oppression of a resident alien has had these words added:

> You know the heart of an alien, for you were aliens in the land of Egypt. (Exod 23:9)

Three times in Part II the reader of the law, or the listener, is reminded of an exodus experience from Egypt.[24] Words of explanation and exhortation following apodictic laws in Part II are all later additions to the code. It is also possible that passages that identify Yahweh as the speaker are later additions to an early, leaner code.

Part II differs from Part I in the following ways: (a) Apodictic laws predominate. (b) Some laws are related to the cult of Yahweh. (c) The voice of a divine being is sometimes present. (d) Frequently laws are accompanied by motive clauses, exhortation, and encouraging words explaining why the law should be kept.

The Cultic Epilogue

In the epilogue we have cultic laws, the first concerning the weekly sabbath. It is our suggestion that the law before the weekly sabbath, concerning the sabbatical year of rest for the land every seven years, was not originally a cultic law but a recommended agricultural principle. Observance of the sabbath year would later become a cultic law and appears in cultic language in Leviticus 25:1–7. The law concerning the sabbatical year ended Part II. It should be stated that allowing the land to lie fallow one year out of seven would not be adequate to produce the hoped-for benefit, restoring the productivity of the soil.[25]

The observance of a weekly sabbath may illustrate the blending of secular and cultic law.

> Six days you shall do your work, but on the seventh day you shall rest. (Exod 23:12)

Following this apodictic law there is a hortative explanation tying the purpose of the law to a humanitarian motive. Not only do you need a day of rest, but your servants along with resident aliens are entitled to a day of rest along with your farm animals. This explanation is in harmony with the editorial words following the sabbath command in the version of the Ten Commandments appearing in Deuteronomy (5:12–15). The Deuteronomy motive clause goes further, however, and ties sabbath observance to a period of bondage in Egypt.[26] We will discuss the Deuteronomic Law Code in chapter 3. But notice two things: (1) *weekly worship* is not required by the sabbath; and (2) the sabbath in the cultic epilogue is not tied to the creation of the world in six days, with Elohim resting on the seventh, as it is in the Ethical Decalogue of Exodus 20:2–17.

One further observation concerning the cultic laws of the epilogue: All six laws of the epilogue appear in the book of Deuteronomy, while none of the four cultic laws of the prologue appears in Deuteronomy.

Historicization of Agricultural Festivals

Following the sabbath law in the epilogue (Exod 23:14–17) the three mandatory annual festivals are recorded. It should be noted that the spring festival is called the feast of unleavened bread, and no mention is made of the passover. In other locations in the Pentateuch the spring festival is called passover (See Deut 16 for example, and Num 28:16). Also, in the epilogue the second festival is called harvest and first fruits (Exod 23:16). In Numbers and Deuteronomy it is called the festival of weeks. The third festival is called

---

**THE THREE ANNUAL FESTIVALS
IN THE COVENANT CODE**

CHART 2e

1. The spring festival is called unleavened bread. There is no mention of passover as in Numbers 28 and Deuteronomy 16.

2. The second festival is called harvest. Elsewhere it is called weeks (Deut 16:19; Lev 23:15).

3. The third festival is called ingathering. Elsewhere it is called booths (Deut 16:13; Lev 23:34).

4. Only males participate in the three festivals. Elsewhere (in scripture) wives, children, and male and female servants also participate (see Deut 16:14).

ingathering. In Numbers and Deuteronomy it is also called the festival of booths. There is general agreement among scholars that the three festivals were Canaanite agricultural events that were later historicized by priests of the cult of Yahweh. An example of historicization is the explanation of the festival of booths. This explanation dates to the exile or post-exilic period. In Leviticus 23:42–43 we read:

> You shall live in booths for seven days…so that your generations may know that I made the people of Israel live in booths when I brought them out of the land of Egypt.

Boiling a Kid in Its Mother's Milk

The last apodictic law is interesting because the entire series of kosher dietary laws that requires the separation of meat and dairy products is based on this obscure law.

You shall not boil a kid in its mother's milk. (Exod 23:19)

What does this mean? If we take it at face value, it seems to be saying that it is permissible to boil a kid in milk (in which case it certainly would not support separation of meat and dairy), but not its *mother's* milk.[27] In our age of animal rights we are tempted to see an ironic taboo related to compassion, but the original meaning is lost in antiquity. The same law appears in Deuteronomy 14:21 and also in Exodus 34:26, where it ends the so-called Ritual Decalogue.[28]

Summary

Since the two priesthoods of Judah (primarily two) that produced the scrolls of the Hebrew Bible had theological goals, they produced theological histories. They also produced theological law collections and presented them as if they came from the hand (if not the mouth) of God.

By separating Part I of the Covenant Code (Exod 21:1—22:17) from Part II, we see that we have preserved for us in Part I a portion of a completely secular law code. The prologue consisting of four cultic laws misleads us by putting cultic matters before Part I. We may not be able to pinpoint the origin of Part I, but it is reasonable to believe that Part I is a law code that did not originate either with Aaronid or Levitical priests. It was produced by a circle of civic leaders, perhaps lawyers, if you will, or at the very least community leaders with legal minds. They may have been religious, but the collection they put together (of which we only have a portion) did not have a theological theme. This collection contained no reference to Yahweh as an originator of law, and the voice of Yahweh was not heard.

If the priests in Babylonian captivity (or their descendants) put together the canonical book of Exodus, why did they include the Covenant Code? The answer lies in the respect the priestly scribes seem to have had for the contents of older scrolls that they had in their possession. In producing the Tetrateuch (and later adding Deuteronomy to the Tetrateuch to make it a Pentateuch) the scribes of the priestly party demonstrated that they would rather include too much material than make decisions concerning the elimination of written scrolls, or portions of written scrolls, even when the inclusion produced apparent contradictions.

Index to Laws
of the Covenant Code
(Exodus 20:22—23:19)

(Sorted by a key word in each law)

3

The Law Code of Deuteronomy
Deuteronomy 12—16

> These are the statutes and ordinances that you must diligently observe
> in the land that the LORD your God…has given you. (Deut 12:1)

The Deuteronomic law code is located at the core of the canonical book of
Deuteronomy, chapters 12—26. The book of Deuteronomy is the only book
of the Bible that grew from the center out. The circle of scribes that produced the scroll of Deuteronomy over a period of changing times for
Israel/Judah added several new beginnings and endings to Deuteronomy in
accordance with emerging theological understanding based on an idealized
relationship between Israel and Yahweh. (In the Hebrew Bible this scroll is
named *Debarim.*)[1]

The growth of Deuteronomy took place from the last decades of
Judah's existence as an independent political entity (621–586 B.C.E.), into
the exilic period, and ended sometime during the restoration period in post-
exilic Judah (called by the Persians Yehud). The following three sentences
may have been sequential openings for the scroll as it grew in stages:

> Hear O Israel: The LORD is our God, the LORD alone. (Deut 6:4)

> This is the law that Moses set before the Israelites. (Deut 4:44)

and finally

> These are the words that Moses spoke to all Israel beyond the Jordan.
> (Deut 1:1)

The canonical opening (1:1) was part of a three-chapter segment added to a previous edition of the scroll to connect Deuteronomy to the Tetrateuch. Notice that all three openings are concerned with *the words of the law.*

The Legal Portion of Deuteronomy

The collection of law found in Deuteronomy—the Deuteronomic Code—is located in chapters 12 through 26. The Deuteronomic Code is a mosaic (excuse the pun) of many apparently diverse pieces. There are laws covering a surprisingly large range of subjects including Yahweh's chosen place, annual festivals, pillars, sacred poles, prophets, farming, farm animals, marriage, slaves, Levites, disposition of body waste, soldiers, aliens, the rich and the poor, the administration of justice, and a parapet on the roof of a house. When these diverse pieces are viewed as a whole, they portray for us a fascinating idealized Israel. This law collection is a mixture of lofty spirituality, everyday practicality, and concern for societal justice, interspersed with exhortation and encouragement supplied by its Levitical authors and editors. Alongside high-minded ethical demands are impractical statutes and requirements that if carried out could only be described as inhuman and cruel. For example, read chapter 13 in its entirety, where violent remedies are legalized and demanded as punishment for treason against the Lord.[2] In one case the destruction of a whole town that has been led astray is required:

> You shall put the inhabitants of that town to the sword, utterly destroying it and everything in it—even putting its livestock to the sword. (Deut 13:15)

Of course, we should be aware that there is not one recorded example throughout the history of Israel when the above law (concerning the destruction of the people and livestock because the town turned from the worship of Yahweh) was enforced or carried out.[3]

Because portions of the Deuteronomic Code differ in content, form, and style, we may conclude that the Deuteronomic Code is the result of editorial activity which, as time passed, enlarged it with both individual laws and small collections of laws from various sources. This is also true of the other law collections that appear in the Pentateuch.

Was This the Book of the Law Discovered in the Temple?

While it is widely believed that the book of the law discovered in the temple during the reign of Josiah was the core of the book of Deuteronomy, it is probable that the law code read to Josiah by Shaphan the secretary, and

LAW CATEGORIES IN THE DEUTERONOMIC CODE
(DEUTERONOMY 12—26)

Chapter

12 Destruction of Canaanite high places including altars, pillars, poles, posts, and idols (vv. 2–4)

Acceptable worship of Yahweh alone at Yahweh's chosen place for his name to dwell (v. 5)

Presentation of sacrifices, offerings, tithes, donations and gifts, and observation of annual pilgrimage feasts must occur only at the chosen place (vv. 6–7, 11–18, 26–27)

Secular slaughter of meat permissible; consumption of blood forbidden (vv. 15–16, 20–25)

13 Apostasy of prophets (vv. 1–5), individuals (vv. 6– 11), towns (vv. 12–18)

14 Clean, unclean foods (vv. 3–21) and tithes (vv. 22–29)

15 Sabbatical year: release of debts (vv. 1–11), slaves (vv. 12–18); firstborn of livestock (vv. 19–23)

16 Three annual pilgrimage festivals
    Passover (vv. 1–8)
    Weeks (vv. 9–12)
    Booths (vv. 13–17)
Judges and officials (vv. 18–20)

17 Forbidden forms of worship (vv. 2–7)
Legal decision-makers (vv. 8–13)
Laws for king (vv. 14–20)

18 Levites (vv. 1–8), abhorrent practices (vv. 9–14), prophets (vv. 15–22)

19 Cities of refuge (vv. 1–11), boundary marker (v. 14), witnesses (vv. 15–21)

20 Rules of warfare (vv. 1–20)

21 Murder by person unknown (vv. 1–9), female captives (vv. 10–14), firstborn rights (vv. 15–17), rebellious children (vv. 18–21), hanging (vv. 22–23)

22 Neighbor's livestock (1–4); miscellaneous subjects: apparel, mother bird, parapet, forbidden mixing, tassels (5–12); sexual relations (13–30)

23 Exclusions from the assembly (vv. 1–7)
Clean camp (vv. 9–14)

Miscellaneous: escaped slaves, temple prostitutes, interest on loans, vows, eating from neighbor's fields (vv. 15–25)

24 A divorced wife (vv. 1–4)

Miscellaneous: newly married soldier, a millstone as a pledge, kidnapping, skin disease, lending to a neighbor, wages for day laborers, persons only responsible for their own crimes, justice for aliens and orphans, harvest guidelines (vv. 5–21)

25 Flogging (vv. 1–4); levirate marriage (vv. 5–10), weights and measures (vv. 13–16)

26 First fruits and liturgy (vv. 1–11), tithes and liturgy (vv. 12–15)

later read by Josiah to *all the people of Judah* (2 Kgs 23:2, emphasis added), was shorter than the code that now comprises chapters 12—26 of Deuteronomy. In other words the law code itself (chapters 12–26) grew in size and content as the book of Deuteronomy grew in stages with additions of new beginnings and endings.

The Number of Laws in the Deuteronomic Code

There is no agreement among scholars about how the individual laws of the Deuteronomic Code should be divided, so the total count differs. Jewish tradition states that 174 laws make up the code.[4] In a popular Christian commentary the number of laws is reported as 78.[5] Our count is 127. At any rate, the Deuteronomic Code is more than four times the length of the Covenant Code, which contains 52 brief laws. Only 19 of the laws of the Covenant Code appear in the Deuteronomic Code (see Chart 3a).

**COVENANT CODE LAWS THAT APPEAR
IN THE DEUTERONOMIC LAW CODE
(BY SECTION)**

CHART 3a

Prologue:	None of the four cultic laws appears in the Deuteronomic Code.
Part I:	Only four of the twenty-two mostly casuistic laws appear in the Deuteronomic Code.
Part II:	Only nine of the twenty apodictic (unconditional) laws (often with exhortative language) based on a divine demand for justice appear in the Deuteronomic Code.
Epilogue:	All six cultic laws, including required participation in three annual festivals, appear in Deuteronomy.

The Deuteronomic Code contains fewer laws than the Holiness Code (Lev 17—26), which by our count numbers 161 laws, but is longer in wordage by 10 percent. We will discuss the Holiness Code in chapter 4.

The Historical Role of the Deuteronomic Code

Because the Deuteronomic Code is last in the Pentateuch and follows the Covenant Code and the Holiness Code, not to mention the scattered portions of the Priestly Code and several summaries of laws (like the decalogues), it is important that we reorient our thinking about the Deuteronomic Code and the circle that produced it in its earliest form. It is our belief that the code was the product of the Deuteronomic circle. This circle was made up of levitical priests and traced its origin to the Shechem/Shiloh area of the northern kingdom of Israel. When reading the literary output of the Deuteronomic circle, we notice that its authors present themselves as conservative protectors of ancient values and beliefs. But this was not the true picture. The truth is that this circle was made up of innovative, ground-breaking thinkers who were on the cutting edge of theological innovation. During the reign of Josiah they were involved in the replacement of fragmented, outdated perceptions of Yahweh with a new concept that would forever change the religion of Judah. At the center of this new conception was a new theological understanding. For the first time Yahweh was presented to the people as a God preoccupied with observance of law.[6] The reason it is difficult for the student to grasp this is because the entire Deuteronomic History (Joshua, Judges, Samuel, Kings) was written to support this Josianic view of Yahweh. When we read the Deuteronomic Code we are reading an enlarged version of the first law collection (historically) in which Yahweh had a personal investment.

Justice Themes in the Deuteronomic Code

A hortatory tone permeates the Torah of Deuteronomy. This exhortative quality has been referred to by scholars as "the law preached."[7] Readers of the Deuteronomic Torah are frequently encouraged to keep the law by the narrator or editor. For example, after the law requiring the release of slaves after six years of service, the following encouragement is given:

> Do not consider it a hardship when you send them out from you free persons, because for six years they have given you services worth the wages of hired laborers; and the LORD your God will bless you in all that you do. (Deut 15:18)

This type of encouragement or exhortation does not appear in any of the other collections of law in the Torah—the Covenant Code, the Holiness Code, or the Priestly Code.

The subject of the Deuteronomic Torah, unlike the Holiness Code and the Priestly Code, is human relations, responsibility, cooperation, and interdependence. It becomes obvious, when the contents of the codes are compared, that two entirely different theological schools are involved. As we shall see, the Aaronid priests produced a code preoccupied with animal sacrifice, blood, cleanness, uncleanness, and concern for something called holiness. The book of Leviticus, representative of this non-Deuteronomic theology, is the product of the Aaronid priesthood.

It is obvious that the Deuteronomic Torah is dependent to some extent on older sections of the previously discussed Covenant Code. There is a difference, however. In the Deuteronomic Code the laws are frequently reworded and made more humane. A prime example of this is the law of the Hebrew slave. In Exodus it reads, in part:

> When you buy a male Hebrew slave, he shall serve six years, but in the seventh he shall go out a free person, without debt....If his master gives

him a wife and she bears him sons or daughters, the wife and her children shall be her master's and he [the slave] shall go out alone. (Exod 21:2–6)

When the same law appears in Deuteronomy, we see several significant changes: (1) In the earlier law only the male debt slave is set free. In Deuteronomy both a female and a male debt slave are set free (Deut 15:17–18). (2) In Exodus the debt slave receives freedom, but no provision. Deuteronomy states:

> When you send a male slave out from you a free person, you shall not send him out empty-handed. Provide liberally out of your flock, your threshing floor, and your wine press, thus giving to him some of the bounty with which the LORD your God has blessed you....You shall do the same with regard to your female slave. (Deut 15:13–14, 17)

(3) In Exodus the debt slave must leave his wife and children behind *if the master provided the wife.* In Deuteronomy no mention is made of the master providing a wife. The family of the debt slave is only his business. (4) In Exodus the employer is called a master five times (Exod 21:4–8). In Deuteronomy the word *master* is not used.

Here are other examples of the humanizing of law and the move in the direction of social justice found in the Deuteronomic Code:

(1) In Exodus a Hebrew father can sell his daughter as a slave (Exod 21:7). There is no such law in Deuteronomy. In Deuteronomy a daughter can initiate a debt slave agreement on her own, however. (2) In Exodus the law concerning the forced seduction of an un-engaged virgin is concerned with the loss of the father's bride-price *[mohar]* (Exod 22:16–17), not the plight of the young woman. In Deuteronomy (22:28) a violated virgin who becomes a wife cannot be divorced. The Deuteronomic version of the law is concerned with the protection of the violated woman, not the father's bride-price. (3) In Exodus only males make pilgrimages three times a year (Exod 23:17). In the Deuteronomic Code wives and daughters are included (Deut 16:11 and 16:14). (4) In Exodus the oppression of a resident alien is forbidden (Exod 23:9), but in Deuteronomy the Israelite is commanded to love the alien (10:19).[8] (5) In Exodus an animal that is not properly slaughtered is given to the dogs (Exod 22:31). In Deuteronomy, where hunger is considered, the animal can be given to a non-Israelite.

We should also note that in Deuteronomy the reason for keeping the sabbath day is humanitarian. Every worker and every farm animal is entitled to a day of rest (5:14–15). In Exodus the reason given for keeping the sabbath is tied to the creation myth that God created the world in six days and rested on the seventh.

**IN THE DEUTERONOMIC CODE THE POOR
AND POWERLESS ARE PROTECTED**

CHART 3b

- Male and female slaves are freed the seventh year and must be generously provisioned to start their new lives. (15:12–18)

- Widows, the fatherless, and the sojourner must be provided for at annual festivals and at harvest times. (16:11, 14; 24:19–22)

- Female prisoners of war have rights and must be treated with respect. (21:10–14)

- Slaves who run from their owners are not to be returned to their owners. (23:15–16)

- Israelites who because of setbacks must borrow are not to be charged interest on money, provisions, or anything. (23:15)

- If there are any in need, the code commands that one not be hardhearted or tightfisted: "Open your hand, willingly lending enough to meet the need whatever it may be" (15:8)

The Voice of God

While we maintain that Yahweh was preoccupied with law in the Deuteronomic Code, we cannot help but notice that Yahweh does not speak. The words are the words of Moses. We pointed out in our discussion of the Covenant Code that the cultic laws and certain laws of Part II (apodictic laws) had a first-person speaker, Yahweh. For example,

You shall not go up by steps *to my altar.* (Exod 20:26, emphasis added)

No one shall appear *before me* empty-handed. (Exod 23:15, emphasis added)

In the Deuteronomic Code Yahweh is spoken of in the third person. Compare the wording that prefaces the three annual festivals. In the Covenant Code we read "Three times a year you will hold a festival *for me.*" In the Deuteronomic Code the words prefacing the three annual festivals are in the third person: "Three times a year all your males shall appear before the LORD your God." In the Covenant Code God is the speaker; in the Deuteronomic Code Moses is the speaker. Only a few times are the words of God quoted in the Deuteronomic Code:

> The LORD has said to you, "You must never return that way again." (Deut 17:16)

> Then the LORD replied to me "They are right in what they have said. I will raise up for them a prophet like you from among their own people." (Deut 18:17–18)

Centralization of Yahweh Worship

The first and basic law of the Deuteronomic Code requires that Yahweh be worshiped only at one location, the place chosen by Yahweh for his name to dwell (Deut 12:5–12).

> Take care that you do not offer your burnt offerings at any place you happen to see. But only at the place that the LORD will choose in one of your tribes—there you shall offer your burnt offerings and there you shall do everything I command you. (Deut 12:13)

In the first twelve laws of the Deuteronomic Code the place chosen by Yahweh is mentioned four times (vv. 5–7, 11–14, 18, 26). This command for centralized worship is considered the heart of the code, the basic Deuteronomic law. Centralization was not included in the Covenant Code, which implied that there would be multiple altars:

> In every place where I cause my name to be remembered I will come to you and bless you. (Exod 20:24)

In spite of the fact that the centralization law is basic to the Deuteronomic Code, it is surprising that there is no mention of a central structure: a tent of meeting, a tabernacle, or a temple.

It is generally believed that in the Holiness Code the centrality of one legitimate altar is assumed and is referred to as the "tent" or the "tent of meeting." In the Priestly Code the one authorized place of worship is assumed to be the place where the Aaronid priests (the sons of Aaron) are established to carry out their appointed activities, referred to repeatedly as the "tabernacle." Scholars generally point out that before the monarchical period some groups in Israel believed that Shiloh was the chosen place for the worship of Yahweh.

> Shiloh, where I made my name dwell at first. (Jer 7:12)

References to the tabernacle in the Priestly Code constantly recur, but the word *tabernacle* (singular) does not appear once in the Deuteronomic Code.

We are quick to state, inaccurately, that the Deuteronomic Code established the one centralized official shrine for the worship of Yahweh. However, if we read the opening of the code carefully, keeping in mind that the temple in Jerusalem was already a central, official shrine[9] when the Deuteronomic Code was *discovered,* we realize that the Deuteronomic Code is primarily *eliminating,* prohibiting all other altars and shrines throughout Judah and Israel:

> You must demolish completely all the places where the nations…served their gods, on the mountain heights, on the hills, and under every leafy tree. Break down their altars, smash their pillars, burn their sacred poles with fire, and hew down the idols of their gods, and thus blot out their names from their places. (Deut 12:2–3)[10]

There are many laws and ordinances in the Deuteronomic Code that do not mention the concept of centralization. In a commentary on Deuteronomy, Gerhard von Rad writes:

> There are after all a large number of ordinances which neither mention the demand for centralization nor seem to be at all aware of it.[11]

The uniqueness of the Deuteronomic Code will become more obvious to us as we discuss the content of the Holiness Code. In comparison with the much shorter Covenant Code note that the word *ox* appears twenty-one times. In the Deuteronomic Code it appears only seven times. The four cultic laws in the prologue of the Covenant Code do not appear in the Deuteronomic Code. In fact, the cultic law that mentions "every place where I cause my name to be remembered" (Exod 20:24) is not in harmony with the primary law of the Deuteronomic Code, which stresses the centrality of the one place chosen by Yahweh for the location of the one central altar (Deut 12:5, 11, 18).

When comparing the Deuteronomic Code with the other law collections of the Pentateuch, we discover the distinguishing characteristics of the Deuteronomic Code that we have listed in Chart 4c. It contains laws that are unique to itself and omits laws that appear to be central in other collections. There is no specific listing of laws concerning offerings such as we find in the Priestly Code:

> This is the ritual of the burnt offering, the grain offering, the sin offering, the guilt offering, the offering of ordination, and the sacrifice of well-being, which the LORD commanded Moses on Mount Sinai. (Lev 7:37–38)[12]

UNIQUE ASPECTS OF THE DEUTERONOMIC CODE (DEUTERONOMY 12—26)

CHART 3c

1. There is a primary and specific emphasis on the centralization of Yahweh's shrine, the one approved place chosen by Yahweh (12:5–7, 16:2, 11, 15). The phrase "the place that he [Yahweh] will choose" appears twenty times. This expression does not appear in the Covenant Code or the Holiness Code.

2. Secular (profane) slaughter for consumption of meat at home is specifically permitted (12:15, 20–22).

3. There are laws related to a king (17:14–20).

4. Prophets are mentioned (13:1–5; 18:15–22).

5. The name theology appears throughout. For example, the passover must be observed "at the place that the LORD your God will choose as a dwelling *for his name*" (16:6, emphasis added).

6. All priests are Levites, and all Levites can be priests (18:1–8). Contrast Num 3:1–10.

7. Priests in the Deuteronomic Code are never called *the sons of Aaron* as they are repeatedly in both the Holiness Code (Lev 17:2; 22:2,18) and the Priestly Code throughout (for example, Exod 30:19; Lev 3:13; Num 3:10).

8. There are no regulations for priests such as those found in the Holiness Code (Lev 21, for example).

9. The laws of the Deuteronomic Code are repeatedly interspersed with hortatory material explaining the reason for the law and encouraging the keeping of the law. The expression "so that Yahweh may bless you" appears five times.

10. There are laws concerning the conduct of war (Deut 20:1–20; 23:9–14).

11. Only in Deuteronomy do we find commands to *love* God. This requirement does not appear in any other collection of biblical law.

12. The Deuteronomic Code proper (Deut 12—26) contains no requirement for observance of a weekly sabbath (day of rest).

13. There is no requirement for circumcision (Lev 12:3).

14. There is no mention of Yom Kippur, a day of atonement (Lev 23:26–32).

15. The word *holy* appears only six times in the Deuteronomic Code. In the Holiness Code the word *holy* appears forty-one times and has a different meaning.

16. The word *tabernacle* (singular) does not appear in the Deuteronomic Code.

17. Only in the Deuteronomic Code is there mention of the third year as the year of the tithe (Deut 26:12). The theological term *tithe* appears nine times in the Deuteronomic Code. It does not appear in the Covenant Code or the Holiness Code.

18. The Deuteronomic Code is the only law collection that mandates liturgical responses from worshipers. This happens several times; once the response begins with the words, "A wandering Aramean was my ancestor" (Deut 26:5), and again, beginning with the words, "I have removed the sacred portion from the house" (Deut 26:13).

There is a relative lack of interest in the Deuteronomic Code concerning priestly activity, an interest that dominates the Holiness Code and the Priestly Code. In the Deuteronomic Code there is no mention of Yom Kippur, the day of atonement, no requirement for a weekly sabbath,[13] or day of rest, and no requirement for circumcision of male infants. Also the word *tabernacle* does not appear. On the other hand, the Deuteronomic Code contains laws that do not appear in other codes, such as laws related to the conduct of wars, kings, and prophets. And, surprisingly, only the Deuteronomic Code mentions the requirement to *love* Yahweh (Deut 13:3).

**THE THREE ANNUAL FESTIVALS
IN THE DEUTERONOMIC CODE
(DEUTERONOMY 16:1–17)**

CHART 3d

1. (a) The spring festival is called passover. Unleavened bread is mentioned twice.

   (b) In the Book of the Covenant the spring festival is described in one sentence. In the Deuteronomic Code there are nine sentences (Deut 16:1–8).

   (c) In the Deuteronomic Code observance of the festival is forbidden in "any of your towns." In the Book of the Covenant the location for observance of the spring festival is unclear.

2. The festival of weeks shall be observed seven weeks from the time the sickle is first put to the standing grain. (In the Book of the Covenant the festival is called harvest.)

3. (a) The festival of booths will be observed when you have gathered in the produce from your threshing floor and your wine press.

   (b) There is no historicization of booths in the Deuteronomic Code as is found in Holiness Code (Lev 23:43–44).

   (c) In the Book of the Covenant the third festival is called ingathering. The word *booths* does not appear.

   Following the description of the three annual festivals there is a statement that three times a year "all your males shall appear before the LORD" (Deut 16:16). This instruction conflicts with another statement of the Deuteronomic Code that includes sons and daughters, male and female slaves, Levites, strangers, orphans, and widows in the observation of the annual festivals (see Deut 16:11 and 16:14).

   All three festivals must be observed only at the place Yahweh chooses.

Truth as the Product of Intrinsic Tension

To the student familiar with the many ways in which the Deutero-nomic Code differs from the other three law codes it is obvious that the Hebrew Bible is the product of contrasting theologies and views of religion promoted by different priesthoods and that the viewpoints of these contrast-ing schools grew and transformed themselves in response to changing politi-cal, economic, and social developments. One of the great characteristics of biblical truth is that it is the end product of tensions that are as relevant today as they were during the period when they were first recorded. Becom-ing familiar with the laws of Deuteronomy as contrasted with the laws of Leviticus, for example, enables us to be more articulate in the area of theo-logical tension. With this in mind we move in chapter 4 to a discussion of the Holiness Code.

Index to Laws
of the Deuteronomic Code
(Deuteronomy 12—26)
(Sorted by a key word in each law)

4

The Holiness Code
Leviticus 17—26

You shall be holy, for I the LORD [Yahweh] your God am holy. (Lev 19:2)

We have heard the above words many times, and thus we may be immune to the unique theological concept they embody. We do not know the precise time when the priests of the Jerusalem temple started to believe and to teach that Yahweh was holy, but it cannot be a coincidence that the favorite name for God of the earliest historical prophet of Jerusalem, Isaiah, was "the holy one of Israel." And we remember that Isaiah's call took place in the temple, where Isaiah heard the words *"Holy, holy, holy is the LORD of hosts* (Isa 6:3).

In 1877 the biblical scholar August Klostermann recognized the power of this concept (holiness) and was able to identify a distinct law collection of which this law was a key. This collection begins in Leviticus 17 and ends with Leviticus 26. Klostermann gave the name Holiness Code to this collection, and it has been widely, almost universally accepted.[1] Klostermann noted that the Holiness Code was characterized by a hortatory tone and that its laws combined an emphasis on cultic purity with moral behavior.

The Hebrew word for holy, *qadosh,* has to do with being separate and apart. Of course the word *holy* embodies something more than simple separateness, demanding ceremonial cleanness of persons, places, and objects.[2] Frank Crusemann writes of the *"electric field* of the holy with its positive and negative possibilities."[3]

While holiness often can be understood as nothing more than ceremonial cleanliness, Susan Ackermann reminds us of the negative side of holiness, which is often associated with cult items and other sacred things and places: "In 2 Samuel 6:6–11 Uzzah dies because he touches the ark,

killed by the holiness the cult object communicates....Holiness is danger-
ous; holiness destroys."[4]

The Holiness Code, like the Covenant Code and the Deuteronomic
Code, is bracketed by laws. At its beginning is the proper place (altar) for
animal sacrifices to Yahweh (Lev 17:1–8); it concludes with a promise concerning blessings for keeping the law (Lev 26:3–13). Like the Deuteronomic
Code (Deut 27:11–26; 28:15–68), the Holiness Code also contains the threat
of curses for ignoring the law (Lev 26:14–26).

HOLINESS CODE HIGHLIGHTS

CHART 4a

Chapter

17 Law banning secular slaughter; absolute restriction concerning
the eating of blood.

18 Sexual taboos; because of these abominations the land vomited
out the previous inhabitants.

19 Laws for the people (not the priests); most of these laws are ethi-
cal/secular as opposed to cultic.

20 A repetition of the sexual taboo laws of chapter 18 with several
penalties.

21 Laws pertaining to the lives of the priests.

22 Laws pertaining to the eating of sacred donations; who may eat
sacred donations; what makes an acceptable sacrificial offering.

23 Appointed annual festivals: passover, unleavened bread; first fruits
of harvest; festival of trumpets; Yom Kippur; festival of booths.

24 Lampstand and its oil; bread for the sons of Aaron; narrative of a
blasphemer put to death in which is embedded six laws concerning maiming and killing.

25 Complete rest for the land every seven years; the fiftieth year shall
be a year of jubilee.

26 Blessings for keeping the law; curses for not keeping the law; if
dispersed people repent God will remember his covenant.

But the Holiness Code goes further than simply stressing the holiness of Yahweh and his priests. The people of Yahweh must also be holy.

> The LORD spoke to Moses saying: Speak to all the congregation of the people of Israel and say to them: You shall be holy, for I the LORD your God am holy. (Lev 19:1–2)

The idea that the people of a holy God can and must also be holy contains the seeds of a powerful theological supposition, perhaps unique in the ancient world.

There are three circles or realms of holiness in the Holiness Code. At the core is a God who is the essence of holiness; the next concentric circle consists of the priests and the place of God's dwelling;[5] and then the people of Yahweh form a vast circle of holiness, worshiping and honoring God through the agency and mediation of the priests, the sons of Aaron.

The Relationship of the Priestly Code to the Holiness Code

We will be discussing the Priestly Code in chapter 5, but we should say a word about the relationship between the Holiness Code and the Priestly Code. It is our belief that the Priestly Code in its pre-exilic form was originally a private manual for the priests of the Jerusalem temple meant to be used for the preservation and perpetuation of priestly procedures from generation to generation. Before the Priestly Code became part of the Tetrateuch, it was read and studied by Aaronid priests and was not intended to be used at public readings.

The Holiness Code (as a scroll separate from the Priestly Code) was first produced by Aaronid priests who decided that the priests of the temple should play an active role in the education of the people of Judah. For this reason the Holiness Code contains secular non-cultic laws that had not appeared in the Priestly Code. Thus we are suggesting that the Holiness Code was created for public reading by a circle of Aaronids, priests familiar with the Priestly Code, who combined cultic laws and secular, ethical laws for the spiritual and moral education of the people of Judah.[6]

The Opening Law of the Holiness Code

It is important to note the law that opens the Holiness Code. In summary, this law forbids the secular sacrifice of animals. No one is permitted to slaughter an animal in an open field or outside the camp, or even in the camp.[7]

EXAMPLES OF CULTIC LAWS IN THE HOLINESS CODE (LEVITICUS 17—26)

CHART 4b

Holy Days and Festivals

• Passover and festival of unleavened bread	23:5–8
• Requirements for the festival of weeks	23:15–21
• Festival of trumpets	23:23–25
• Requirements for the day of atonement	23:26–32
• Requirements for the festival of booths	23:33–42

Animal Sacrifices

• Slaughtered animal must be a sacrifice to God	17:3–4
• Animal with blemish excluded as an offering	22:18–20
• Animal with injury excluded as an offering	22:21–25
• Sacrifices to goat-demons forbidden	17:7
• Sacrifice of well-being requirements	19:5–8
• Sacrifices in an open field forbidden	17:5

Instructions for Priests

• They shall not make bald spots on their heads	21:5
• They shall not trim the edges of their beards	21:5
• A priest with blemish shall not make an offering	21:17
• Blemishes that eliminate a priest	21:16–20
• They may prepare corpse of kin	21:1–4
• They shall not marry a divorced woman	21:7
• They shall be holy to their God	21:6
• Priests shall eat the bread of the sanctuary	24:5–9

High Priests

• A high priest shall marry a virgin of his own kin	21:13–15
• He shall not go outside the sanctuary	21:12
• He shall not dishevel his hair	21:10
• He shall not tear his vestments	21:10
• He shall not go near a dead body	21:11

> If anyone of the house of Israel slaughters an ox or a lamb or a goat in the camp, or slaughters it outside the camp, and does not bring it to the entrance of the tent of meeting, to present it as an offering to the LORD before the tabernacle of the LORD…he shall be cut off from the people. (17:3–4)

All sacrifices must be brought to the priests at the entrance of the tent of meeting. The understanding of this law and its location in the Holiness Code plays an important role in the scholarly debate concerning the time and place of the code's origin.

The Date for the Origin of the Holiness Code

There is no firm agreement among scholars for the time of origin of the Holiness Code. Some scholars argue that the most logical time for the appearance was during the captivity of a Judahite community in Babylon, 587–39 B.C.E. There are many others who insist that the Holiness Code had to exist in pre-exilic Judah.[8] Let us look at the logic of each position.

A Pre-exilic Origin for the Holiness Code?

Those who argue for a monarchical, pre-exilic origin for the Holiness Code locate it in the late eighth century during the reign of Hezekiah. With its inclusion of social economic laws, the code is believed to be a response to the attacks of the eighth-century social critics (later called prophets) on the economic imbalance of Israelite/Judahite society.

I. Knohl writes:

> HS [the Holiness School] expresses the attempt of priestly circles in Jerusalem to contend with the prophets' criticism. In reaction…HS created the broader concept of holiness that integrates morality and cult and drew up a comprehensive program for social rehabilitation formulated in sacral terms.[9]

Scholars point to the Deuteronomic law that *permits* secular slaughter—

> Whenever you desire you may slaughter and eat meat within any of your towns, according to the blessing that the LORD your God has given you (Deut 12:15)—

as a direct reaction to the Hezekian restriction of the late-eighth-century Holiness Code, which forbade secular slaughter.

CONSIDERING THE GEOGRAPHY OF ANCIENT ISRAEL, HOW WAS IT POSSIBLE TO REQUIRE THAT ALL SLAUGHTERED ANIMALS BE BROUGHT TO THE TENT OF MEETING AS A SACRIFICE TO YAHWEH? (LEVITICUS 17:3–7)

CHART 4c

---

1. If this law appeared before the monarchy, or early in the monarchy, it may have applied to any established shrine with a priest in attendance (symbolized by the tent of meeting) rather than permitting slaughter at an improvised altar (see Jacob Milgrom, "Leviticus," in *The Interpreter's One Volume Commentary on the Bible*, 78).

2. This law may have appeared in Judah at a time when the territory of Judah was quite small and the temple was not far from anyone. For example, this was true following the invasion of Sennacherib in 701 B.C.E. This would have been during the reign of Hezekiah if we accept a termination date for Hezekiah of 687 (see chronology in the *New Jerome Biblical Commentary*, 1233).

3. This law may have originated in Babylon for the small Judahite community in captivity, 587–39 B.C.E. (see Crusemann, *The Torah*, 277–86).

Jan Joosten[10] claims that the Holiness Code was composed for a rural, pastoral people and that this indicates that an exilic origin for the code is highly unlikely. And Jacob Milgrom argues that the Deuteronomic Law Code permitting secular slaughter (Deut 12:20–21) was a reaction to the opening law of the Holiness Code (restricting animal slaughter), which had to exist prior to the appearance of the Deuteronomic Code during the reign of Josiah.[11]

An Exilic Origin for the Holiness Code?

Those who argue for an exilic origin for the code reason more or less as follows. The insistence on the holiness of the congregation of Israel assists us in dating the canonical version of the Holiness Code. This body of law (along with the Priestly Code) teaches the Judahite community in

Babylonian captivity that the people of Yahweh, like Yahweh himself, are separate and unique. A circle of royal priests, formerly of the Jerusalem temple, insisted that Judahites far from home in captivity were nevertheless obligated to maintain their identity as the congregation of Yahweh.

So the goal of the exilic authors of the Holiness Code was twofold: to preserve the necessary role of the priesthood (the sons of Aaron) and to create and preserve the identity of the exiles as the unique people of Yahweh. Cultic laws that preserved the identity of the captives as a separate people included the observation of the seventh day as the sabbath (not stressed in the Josianic collection known as the Deuteronomic Code), strict observance of the day of atonement (also not mentioned in the Deuteronomic Code), and the elimination of secular slaughter in the opening words of the Holiness Code. We know so little about life in captivity for the Jews (597–39 B.C.E.) that we can't say for sure whether there was some kind of a tent shrine in Babylon or whether there was hope among the priesthood that a tent shrine would be established among the captive people at some time. It may have been that the priests were fairly certain of a future return to Judah with an opportunity to rebuild Jerusalem and the temple. In case any among the captives raised a question about the relevancy of the sacred slaughter law in a foreign land, the following words were added:

> This shall be a statute forever to them throughout their generations (Lev 17:7).

Unlike the Priestly Code, the Holiness Code contains ethical, secular laws along with cultic laws (see chart 4e). The circle that produced the exilic expansion of the Holiness Code was influenced by the Deuteronomic Code of the earlier Josianic period. Although the Josianic reform was not a success, the value of the didactic nature of the Deuteronomic Code for the people and its emphasis on non-cultic law had changed the conception of law in Israel forever.

Those who argue for a captivity date for the Holiness Code claim the influence of the Deuteronomic Code on the origin of the Holiness Code. (And those who argue for a *pre-exilic origin* for the Holiness Code claim that there is no demonstrable influence of the Deuteronomic Code on the Holiness Code whatsoever.)

However, a short statement concerning when the Holiness Code appeared can be misleading. As we have pointed out, each law collection contains layers of authorship. So it is possible for the Holiness Code to have appeared in a shorter edition during the pre-exilic period (as a response to prophetic criticism of socioeconomic polarization in society, for example, as stated above) and to have been lengthened and expanded during the exile for reasons totally unrelated to its original purpose. Jacob Milgrom, for example, who maintains that the Holiness Code appeared first during the pre-exilic period, speaks of an H legist who added to the Holiness Code and who lived among the exiles in Babylonia.[12]

Sexual Taboo Laws of Leviticus 18 and 20

The repetition of the list of persons with whom a man cannot have sexual relations is enlightening. First, these holiness laws, like most biblical laws, are addressed only to men (see Chart 4d). Even in the decalogue there is no law that says "Do not covet your neighbor's husband." The fact that the laws are repeated in two lists with different euphemisms for sexual intercourse is a puzzle. We acknowledge that all law collections have layers of authorship, but we wonder why the last editor did not combine the two lists. We are familiar with the combining of disparate written accounts in the narrative sections of the Pentateuch such as the plagues of Exodus and two versions of the flood stories of Genesis. Perhaps the final editor saw enough difference between the two lists (one contains sanctions, punishments) to affect the editor's redactional activity.[13]

The specificity of the listing of these taboo sexual activities assists us in understanding both the respect for and fear of sex in ancient Israel. Tikva Frymer-Kensky of the Reconstructionist Rabbinical College writes:

> Our only indication that the Bible considers sex as volatile, creative, and potentially chaotic force is from the laws themselves. [Sexuality] is a two-edged sword: a force for bonding and a threat to the maintenance of boundaries.[14]

Conclusion

Each law collection of the Torah in its final form contains both cultic (sacred) laws and social (secular) laws. Whether the authors of these collections always meant to differentiate between cultic laws and secular laws we do not know.[15] But it is obvious that the source and subject matter of many of the laws originated separately from and independent of the cult of Yahweh.

The canonical version of the Holiness Code, along with the other law collections of the Torah, contains several layers of authorship. This is most obvious when we compare the sexual taboo laws of Leviticus 18 with those of chapter 20. Ten of the laws found in chapter 18 are repeated in chapter 20. But the euphemism for sexual relations is different. In chapter 18 the expression for sexual relations is "uncover the nakedness of." In chapter 20

**RESTRICTIONS OF SEXUAL RELATIONS THAT APPEAR
TWICE IN THE HOLINESS CODE
(LEVITICUS 18 AND 20)**

CHART 4d

Chapter 18	Chapter 20
You shall not uncover the nakedness of…	You shall not lie with or take…

Chapter 18	Chapter 20
Your father's wife (v. 8)	Your father's wife (v. 11)
Your sister (v. 9)	Your sister (v. 17)
Your father's sister (v. 12)	Your father's sister (v. 19)
Your mother's sister (v. 13)	Your mother's sister (v. 19)
Daughter-in-law (v. 15)	Daughter-in-law (v. 21)
Uncle's wife (aunt) (v. 14)	Uncle's wife (v. 20)
Brother's wife (v. 16)	Brother's wife (v. 21)
A woman and daughter (v. 17)	A mother and daughter (v. 14)
A menstruating woman (v. 19)	A menstruating woman (v. 18)
An animal (v. 23)	An animal (v. 15)

Note: (1) The expressions "uncover the nakedness of," "lie with," and "take" all mean the same thing: to have sexual relations with. (2) The fact that all the above restrictions appear in two separate lists indicates that the Holiness Code is made up of sections of different origins, as is true also of the Covenant Code and the Deuteronomic Code. (3) The restrictions of chapter 20 carry with them punishments, frequently death. This is not true of the same restrictions of chapter 18, where no punishments are specified.

the expression for the same behavior is "lie with" or "take." Also, the restrictions of chapter 20 carry with them punishments, frequently death. This is not true of the same restrictions of chapter 18.

It is possible that the Holiness Code appeared in some form before the exile and was completed, as we have said, during the exile. As we have pointed out, Jacob Milgrom, who maintains that the Holiness Code appeared first during the pre-exilic period, speaks of an H legist who added to the code and who lived among the exiles in Babylonia.[16] Also, a German scholar, C. Feucht, is cited by Hans Boecker as having divided the Holiness Code into two distinct sections.[17] According to this division chapters 18—23

**SUBJECTS OF SECULAR (NON-CULTIC) LAWS
IN THE HOLINESS CODE**

CHART 4e

1.	Commerce and finance	19:11–13, 35–36
2.	Human relationships	19:3, 11–18, 22
3.	Agriculture	23:22
4.	Family relations and marriage	19:3, 20:8, 25:37
5.	Debt slavery	25:13–17, 39, 40–46
6.	Land and houses (real estate)	25:13–17, 23–24, 30–34
7.	Lending and borrowing	25:35–38
8.	Justice issues	19:9–10, 15, 23:22

of Leviticus are believed to predate the discovery of the book of the law and the reform of Josiah, and chapters 25—26 of Leviticus to date from the time of the exile. Finally, numerous affinities of the prophecy of Ezekiel with the Holiness Code are referenced by Lawrence Boadt in his introduction to Ezekiel in the *New Jerome Biblical Commentary.* Father Boadt points out that Ezekiel never ties the priesthood to the house of Aaron, as is done frequently in the Holiness Code.[18]

We cannot close our essay on the Holiness Code without mentioning that although it contains a command to love your neighbor and a command to love the alien, there is no command to love God.

Index to Laws
of the Holiness Code
(Leviticus 17–26)

(Individual laws are listed alphabetically by key words [161 separate laws]. Some laws are indexed by more than one key word.)

5

The Priestly Code

The Priestly Code is the only law collection of the Pentateuch that is not contiguous. Groupings of priestly laws are found scattered throughout Exodus, beginning with chapter 12, occupy much of the book of Leviticus, except for chapters 17 through 26 (a special collection identified as the Holiness Code and discussed previously in chapter 4), and continue in portions of the book of Numbers.[1]

The Priestly Code is chiefly made up of priestly concerns—offerings, sacrifices, festivals, ordinations, vestments, tabernacle construction, tent furnishings and vessels. Some priestly laws are not connected with tabernacle procedures, however. These include laws related to health issues—contagious skin diseases and bodily discharges—Nazirites, inheritance, dietary restrictions, and vows.

The first bundle of priestly laws we encounter is found in Exodus 12—13. Here there are twenty laws, the first eighteen related to passover observance. Two examples:

> You shall keep it [the lamb for passover] until the fourteenth day of this [the first] month; then the whole assembled congregation of Israel shall slaughter it at twilight. (Exod 12:6)

> You shall let none of it remain until the morning. (Exod 12:10)

Following laws in this segment (Exod 12—13) related to passover are two unrelated laws concerning the redemption of a firstborn donkey (Exod 13:13). This law also appears in the Ritual Decalogue, Exodus 34:20.

The next cluster of priestly laws begins in Exodus 25:8 and continues through Exodus 30:37. Between the first and second cluster of priestly laws are the Ethical Decalogue (the Ten Commandments, Exod 20) and the

---

NUMBER OF PRIESTLY LAWS

CHART 5a

Exodus
    Twenty-one laws before the Ten Commandments
      (chapters 12—16)
    Nineteen laws after the Covenant Code (chapters 23—35)

Leviticus
    Seventy-one laws before the Holiness Code
      (chapters 1—16)
    Twelve laws after the Holiness Code (chapter 27)

Numbers
    Fifty-two laws

Note: According to rabbinical tradition there are three laws in Genesis: Gen 1:28;
17:10; and 32:33. If we include the three laws of Genesis as priestly laws, the total number of priestly laws is 178.

Covenant Code (Exod 20:22—23:19). The laws of the second cluster of the Priestly Code are related to priestly activity in a portable sanctuary. Here are two examples:

> And have them [Israel] make me a sanctuary, so that I may dwell among them. (Exod 25:8)

> And you shall set the bread of the Presence on the table before me always. (Exod 25:30)

Notice the word *always* in the law above. While the priestly laws are said to be given to the priests while Israel is in the wilderness, the implication is that these laws are eternal and will apply to a permanent sanctuary in Israel's future. A description of a seven-branched lampstand made of pure beaten gold is found in Exodus 25:31–40. Later, in the description of Solomon's temple found in 1 Kings 6—7, there is no mention of a seven-branched lampstand. Rather there seems to be ten single lampstands (1 Kgs 7:49).

The next cluster of priestly laws is found in Leviticus 1—7. These laws are related to important fixed offerings. At the end of chapter 7 is this summary:

This is the ritual of the burnt offering,[2] the grain offering,…the sin offering, the guilt offering,…and the sacrifice of well-being, which the LORD commanded Moses on Mount Sinai. (Lev 7:37)

Not included in this summary statement, however, are peace offerings and thanksgiving offerings.

The material of sanctuary offerings includes farm animals (a sheep or a goat), trapped birds (turtledoves and pigeons), and produce of various types

MAJOR SUBJECTS OF THE PRIESTLY CODE (EXODUS, LEVITICUS, AND NUMBERS) **CHART 5b**	
Exod 12—13	Laws concerning the festival of passover and unleavened bread.
Exod 25—30	Laws related to the tabernacle
Lev 1—7	Laws related to offerings
Lev 10	Priestly behavior
Lev 11	Dietary laws
Lev 12—15	Laws concerning skin diseases (leprosy) and bodily discharges
Lev 27	Laws concerning vows, offerings, tithes
Num 5—6	Unclean Israelites, unfaithful wives, and Nazirite laws
Num 9—10	Passover laws
Num 18	Priestly laws, Aaronid and Levite
Num 27—30	Inheritance laws, annual festivals, vows
Num 35—36	Levitical towns, laws related to murder, inheritance laws (Zelophehad's daughters)

(fruits and grain). The grain is to be prepared in different ways and is identi-fied as coarse new grain (fresh ears), fine flour, and meal. Everything is spelled out in detail, and there are instructions for cereal offerings that spec-ify cereal or meal fried in oil on a griddle (Lev 6:14), baked in an oven (Lev 7:9), or deep fried in a pot (Lev 7:9). Added to the cooked offerings are oil, frankincense, and salt, and excluded are leaven and honey.

Chapters 8—10 of Leviticus report the ordination of Aaron as the anointed high priest. The mysterious deaths of Aaron's two older sons, Nadab and Abihu, are reported in chapter 10, which is the only true narra-tive in Leviticus.[3] Four laws concerning priestly behavior appear in chapter 10:6–10.

Dietary laws occupy much of chapter 11, with the emphasis on forbid-den nonagricultural food: sea creatures, birds, winged insects, swarming creatures:

> But anything in the seas or the streams that does not have fins and scales, of the swarming creatures in the waters and among all the other living creatures that are in the waters—they are detestable. (Lev 11:10)

> These are unclean for you among the creatures that swarm upon the earth: the weasel, the mouse, the great lizard according to its kind, the gecko, the land crocodile, the lizard, the sand lizard, and the chameleon. (Lev 11:29–30)

Skin Diseases and Bodily Discharges

A peculiarity of the Priestly Code is the laws and procedures involving the priests in the control of both skin diseases and bodily discharges under-stood to be contagious (Lev 13—15).[4]

> When a person has on the skin of his body a swelling or an eruption or a spot, and it turns into a leprous disease on the skin of his body, he shall be brought to Aaron the priest or to one of his sons the priests. (Lev 13:2)

Leviticus 13 contains picturesque detail concerning the diagnosis of infec-tious skin disease. This law determines how a leper will act in society:

> The person who has the leprous disease shall wear torn clothes and let the hair of his head be disheveled; and he shall cover his upper lip and cry out "Unclean, unclean."…He shall live alone; his dwelling shall be outside the camp. (Lev 13:45–46)

In the Deuteronomic History we have no examples of the involvement of Aaronid priests in the control of these diseases. There are several stories of lepers that take place in the northern kingdom.[5] In 2 Chronicles 26 we are told that King Uzziah was leprous in his forehead and therefore lived in a separate house. Priestly laws are referenced in this record.

Although the word *leprosy* is used to describe the skin diseases referred to, we have known for some time that severe leprosy (now known as Hansen's disease) was rare in ancient Israel. The skin disturbances with which the priests dealt in their role as quarantine officials were mostly curable. The role of the royal priests in Jerusalem as ministers of public health grew out of the priestly obsession with the concept of *clean and unclean* and its relationship to holiness. The concern of the priests for the serious threat of skin eruptions to the public health is carried over to genital discharges, as described in Leviticus 15.

Chapter 16 is the last chapter of Leviticus before we encounter the Holiness Code (Leviticus 17—26), where we find no fewer than 164 laws that scholars have identified as a distinct law collection. We have discussed the Holiness Code in the previous chapter. What is interesting about Leviticus 16 is that the word *atonement* appears fifteen times, more than in any other chapter of the Torah, but this is not the chapter that rabbinical tradition cites for the people's requirement to observe Yom Kippur.[6]

Priestly laws continue in the final chapter of Leviticus with twelve laws concerning the exchange value of offerings, vows, and tithes.

The last book containing priestly laws is Numbers, which contains more than fifty laws blended with narrative. In chapters 5 and 6 we find two laws concerning unclean Israelites and several laws dealing with wives suspected of adultery. In chapter 6 there are ten laws dealing with the fulfillment of Nazirite vows and lifestyle. In chapter 9 there are laws concerning the observance of a delayed passover for those who were unclean during the first month.

> In the second month on the fourteenth day, at twilight, they shall keep it [passover]; they shall eat it with unleavened bread and bitter herbs. They shall leave none of it until morning, nor break a bone of it. (Num 9:11–12)

In chapter 15 we find a law concerning tassels:

> Speak to the Israelites, and tell them to make fringes on the corners of their garments throughout their generations. (Num 15:38)

Popular Jewish tradition states that the tassels act like a string around the finger:[7]

> When you see it [the fringe], you will remember the commandments of
> the LORD, and do them, and not follow the lust of your heart and your
> own eyes. (Num 15:39)

In chapter 18 there are nine laws dealing primarily with the duties of
Levites, and in chapters 19 through 30 there are a dozen laws dealing with
various subjects including the uncleanness of a corpse, occasions when additional sacrifices are required, and regulations concerning vows by women.
The most complete cultic calendar is found in Numbers 28—29.

The final laws of the Priestly Code are found in Numbers 35 and have
to do with murder and manslaughter. The most famous law is:

> The evidence of a single witness is not sufficient for putting a person to
> death. (Num 35:30)[8]

THE ANNUAL CULTIC CALENDAR OF NUMBERS 28—29

CHART 5c

1. The spring festival of passover and unleavened bread begins on
   the fourteenth day of the first month. All must abstain from their
   occupations the first day and the seventh day.

2. The festival of weeks, also called first fruits, is to be held annually
   in conjunction with the close of the harvest of grain.

3. On the first day of the seventh month trumpets are blown to
   announce a holy convocation, and special sacrifices and grain
   offerings are required for atonement.

4. On the tenth day of the seventh month a holy convocation is held
   and additional offerings are required.

5. The fifteenth day of the seventh month begins a period of seven
   days (eight according to Numbers 29:35) requiring special sacrifices and offerings. Elsewhere it is called booths (Lev 23:34 and
   Deut 16:13).

The tenth day of the seventh month (no. 4 above) is Yom Kippur, the day of atonement
specified as such in Leviticus 23:27–28 and Leviticus 25:9. Yom Kippur is not mentioned in Numbers or Deuteronomy. Jacob Milgrom suggests that on this day the
people did not go to the temple but stayed home, abstained from work, and afflicted
themselves.[9]

The above summary shows that in the Tetrateuch the laws of the Priestly Code are the first and the last to be encountered.

The Aaronid Priests in Babylonian Captivity

During the Babylonian captivity the first generation of former temple priests initially experienced a decade or more of hopeless disorientation. Far from the location of a destroyed and desecrated Jerusalem, confusion, defeat, and humiliation were the daily diet of the exiled Judean community. Judahites constituted a community wrenched from its homeland and deprived of its king, the temple of its God, and the sacred city of its God's choosing. If there were those among the exiles who believed that some good could come out of the overwhelming despair of their dislocated lives, they were probably few in number.

Much of the credit for the extraordinary recovery and preservation of the Judahite community in captivity belongs to the descendants of the Aaronid royal priesthood and the law code this group generated, along with the other law codes these priests incorporated into their Tetrateuch. Before the exile the royal priests conceived of Yahweh as preoccupied with sacrifices, priestly procedures, and ritual cleanness. For them, the glory *(kabod)* of Yahweh filled the temple as a sign of his presence. In Psalm 135, an Aaronid psalm, Yahweh was said to dwell in Jerusalem.[10]

> O house of Israel, bless the LORD!
>> O house of Aaron, bless the LORD!…
> Blessed be the LORD from Zion,
>> he who resides in Jerusalem. (Ps 135:20–21)

Pre-exilic Aaronid theology had been crushed by the Babylonian invasion. But as decades passed in Babylon, members of the Aaronid priesthood were able to recover and reorganize themselves and engage in leadership activity to meet newly emerging goals. The first of these goals was to assist the Judahite community to survive while maintaining its identity. As time passed, there was the danger that former Judahites would become comfortable, and even prosperous, in their new homes, close to the center of world power.[11] For this reason the formerly royal priests sought to establish a role for themselves within the Judahite community in the light of two possible futures: (1) that there would never be a return to Jerusalem or a new beginning for the destroyed temple, or (2) there would be a return to Jerusalem and the possible reconstruction of the former temple. There are some scholars who believe that the goal of the powerful poetry of Second Isaiah was to persuade second- and third-generation Babylonian Judahites to return to Jerusalem.[12]

With this background information we are able to see the strategy that guided the development of the Aaronid law code. Consider the following:

1. Because the total number of Judahites in Babylon was relatively small (not large enough to support a formerly royal priesthood), deportees were encouraged to be fruitful and multiply.[13]
2. Whatever the status of sabbath observance during the last days of the nation-state of Judah, weekly sabbath observance became a central and key religious practice of the Babylonian community.[14] Sabbath observance was built into the priestly creation account and the priestly explanation of the sabbath commandment in Exodus 20:11.

For in six days the LORD made heaven and earth, the sea, and all that is in them, but rested on the seventh day.[15]

3. Adding to the preservation of Judahite identity was the insistence by the priests of circumcision for all male babies on their eighth day.[16]
4. As a result of witnessing the splendor and pageantry of Babylonian worship, the royal priests recognized the importance of beautiful, meaningful robes and garments for the proper priesthood and incorporated the requirements for priestly attire that we now find in the Priestly Code:[17]

Then bring near to you your brother Aaron, and his sons with him, from among the Israelites, to serve me as priests....When they make these sacred vestments for your brother Aaron and his sons to serve me as priests, they shall use gold, blue, purple, and crimson yarns, and fine linen. (Exod 28:1, 4–5)

5. Insistence on observation of strict dietary laws would contribute to a strong sense of identity for deportees in a foreign country. We cannot say for sure what the status of the dietary laws was in monarchical Judah. Many of the laws may have developed originally as practices of health, but by the time they reached the Torah they were part of the priestly program of holiness (ceremonial cleanness) at all costs.[18]
6. A new national holy day was introduced by the Aaronids, the day of atonement (Lev 16). A day of atonement (Yom Kippur) is unknown in Deuteronomy.
7. In conjunction with the production of an expanded Priestly Law Code, a new literary version of the exodus was produced and fathers were commanded to teach their children the details of this literary version of the exodus experience (Exod 13:8).[19]

Animal Sacrifices

Since so much of the Aaronid Torah deals with animal sacrifices, we should say a word concerning this practice. When the Aaronids went to Babylon, they took with them a manual that they had produced containing regulations and procedures for sacrifices at the Jerusalem temple. More than one hundred of the 613 laws (see chapter 6) deal with animal sacrifices. Moses Maimonides advanced the idea that animal sacrifices were originally instituted to replace the horrible practice of offering human sacrifices to the gods.[20]

In the early decades of captivity sacrifices played a small part in Judahite activity, if any part at all. But after several decades, when the families of the royal Aaronid priests regained their balance, they created their Torah to include explicit laws concerning subjects that would reinforce the identity of Judahites in Babylon as the people of Yahweh. These subjects have been discussed above and include circumcision, sabbath observance, Yom Kippur, dietary laws, and so forth. At the same time the scribes may have expanded and refined the laws concerning sacrifices. Since we know very little about the sacrificial procedures in monarchical Israel, we have to rely on these writings, which may have been idealized during captivity to enhance the need for sacrifices and make the procedures more in accordance with priestly beliefs and expectations. Why would the royal priests do this? Because they had hopes of eventually reinstating the sacrificial system either in Babylon at a tent shrine or in Jerusalem if the opportunity to return and rebuild Jerusalem became a reality.

Sacrifices had been a natural thing for a country that was largely composed of farming and herding families. Once institutionalized by the royal priests, the procedures would continue to survive, centered and controlled in the capital city at the national temple. We have no information concerning the procedures of animal sacrifices at pre-captivity high places, but there are scattered references to animal sacrifice in books containing narrative accounts, such as Genesis, Exodus, and the Deuteronomic History. This brings us to the complicated instructions for the tent shrine that the priests envisioned.

The Tent Shrine

The chronology presented in the canonical scriptures presents the reader with an idealized picture of an ancient community of Israelites, a valuable theological reconstruction that has little basis in history. (Historical Israel did not spend forty years in the wilderness after a miraculous deliverance from Egypt.)[21] The question we must answer is this: From where did the instructions for the building of the tent—including dimensions, materials, specifications for furnishings, and so forth—come? (See Exod 26 and Exod 36—38, for example.)

A logical answer is that the information concerning the tent shrine came from Solomon's temple. And the particularities for Solomon's temple came from Syria and other areas of the ancient Near East. The instructions for the building of the tent shrine in their present form however have been worked over by the Aaronid priests in captivity to conform to a priestly vision of the ideal tent shrine, a description of a shrine made in accordance with a "wish list." (If you could have everything you wanted in a tent shrine, what would you ask for?)

A portable tent shrine may have been envisioned for the Babylonian community of Judahites, a shrine that could be taken apart and transported back to Jerusalem if and when the opportunity presented itself. A rebuilt temple in Jerusalem remained a future hope, but a tent shrine would have to do for the time being. The shrine of the Aaronid torah was a portable shrine. In the canonical wilderness tradition, the Levites would disassemble the shrine when it was time for Israel to move on.

Priestly Laws and Past Events

One of the distinguishing characteristics of the priestly laws is the way they are tied to past events by interweaving them with narrative. For example, the passover laws of Exodus 12—13 are presented as part of the narrative account involving the preparation of the Israelite community on the night of its escape from Egypt. In Leviticus 10 priestly laws follow closely a narrative account of misbehavior on the part of Aaron's sons, Nadab and Abihu. In Numbers the blending of narrative and priestly laws is especially evident in chapters 9—36. In chapter 9 laws concerning passover observance a month late are presented in conjunction with Israel's passover observance one year after the departure from Egypt. In Numbers 18 we find no fewer than nine laws related to priestly concerns, including the duties of Levites and Aaronids:

> You [Aaron] and your sons with you shall diligently perform your priestly duties in all that concerns the altar and the area behind the curtain. (Num 18:7)

> They [Levites] are attached to you in order to perform the duties of the tent of meeting. (Num 18:4)

Shortly following the priestly laws of Numbers 18 we have a narrative account of Aaron's death (Num 20:22–29).

Inheritance laws are presented as part of a narrative concerning Zelophehad's daughters and their inheritance (Num 27, 36).

Not all narrative passages in Numbers are tied to laws, however. There are no laws related to the story of the bronze serpent (Num 21) or to the complex story of Balak summoning Balaam to curse Israel (Num 22—24).[22]

Contribution of the Priestly School

In recent times, as a result of ground-breaking work in form, source, and redaction criticism, first on the part of German scholars, and later by Scandinavian, Dutch, American, and other scholars, the literary contribution of the royal priests in exile has sometimes been negatively evaluated. When it was determined that much of the priestly writings were exilic and did not predate the Deuteronomic school or share the Deuteronomic theology, some scholars began to accuse the priestly circle of rewriting Israelite history, placing too much emphasis on animal sacrifice and other temple activity, insuring their own power over Levitical priests, and not paying enough attention to humanistic matters pertaining to social justice.

It is our view that it is wiser to be more appreciative of the priestly school and its contribution. While it is true that the priests rewrote the history of early Israel, we remember that the Deuteronomists also rewrote the history of Israel, even though they started its history at a later time, after the wilderness experience, with Israel on the verge of entering the land (the book of Joshua). There was nothing new in projecting theology into Israel's past. And it was not unusual for a priesthood to reestablish and expand its own legitimacy.

The day of atonement (Yom Kippur), which the priests conceived of and initiated, has proven its great value and functionality by enduring in Judaism for more than twenty-four-hundred years. The priestly emphasis on ritual, liturgy, vestments, and strict observance of holy days has greatly enriched the culture of Western civilization and has played a vital role in the practices of both Judaism and branches of the Christian church. In many Protestant churches there has been a recent rediscovery of the importance of ritual, vestments, ceremony, and pageantry in the nature and practice of worship.

Index to Laws
of the Priestly Code

(Sorted by a key word in each law)

6

The Rabbinical Tradition of 613 Laws

The word *torah* is used in two ways. In Jewish culture it is used as the name for the sacred scroll containing the five books of Moses. The five books contain both law and narrative. Genesis *(Bereishis)* is entirely narrative, containing only three laws. Rabbinical tradition predating the first century identified the *laws* of the Pentateuch as Torah, giving the word a second, more restrictive meaning. In early Christian writings we have references to the books of Moses as the law:

> On these two commandments hang all the law and the prophets. (Matt 22:40)[1]

When Jesus said:

> "In everything do to others as you would have them do to you; for this is the law and the prophets." (Matt 7:12)

he was referring to the two sections of the Jewish scriptures of his day. The third section, writings *(kethuvim)*, did not become an official part of the canon until later.

The Enumeration of the Laws

The Babylonian Talmud was produced by rabbinical scholars from the third century to the beginning of the sixth century C.E. In this Talmud (there is also another Talmud called the Palestinian Talmud) Rabbi Simlai stated that 613 laws were given to Moses by God, 365 prohibitions corresponding to the number of days in the solar year, and 248 positive commands, the number of parts of the human body.[2] The Talmud does not identify the 613

THE 613 LAWS OF RABBINICAL TRADITION
OF AARON HALEVI
SEFER HA-HINNUCH (THIRTEENTH CENTURY)

CHART 6a

Genesis	3 laws
Exodus	111 laws
Leviticus	247 laws
Numbers	52 laws
Deuteronomy	200 laws
	TOTAL 613 laws

Rabbi HaLevi assembled his listing of 613 laws five centuries before the emergence of higher criticism. There is no recognition of disparate law collections such as the Covenant Code, the Holiness Code, the Deuteronomic Code, or the Priestly Code. The laws are identified in order as they appear in the scrolls of the Torah. (For a breakdown of the distribution of laws in accordance with modern scholarship, see Chart 6b.)

laws, however. Two medieval Jewish scholars have been recognized as having correctly enumerated the 613 laws. They are Moses Maimonides, a twelfth-century Spanish physician, also referred to as Rambam, and Rabbi Aaron HaLevi of Barcelona.

Maimonides arranged the 613 laws into two groups, positive and negative.[3] Aaron HaLevi listed the commandments in the order of their appearance. Before Maimonides enumerated the selection of the 613 laws, there was no universal agreement concerning their identification. Maimonides did not include laws that he considered commands that were not of an everlasting character. However, he did include directions concerning the tabernacle and hallowed food during the wandering of Israel in the wilderness.[4] Maimonides's selection was strenuously argued against by other Rabbis for decades who promoted and defended their own individual selections and classifications.

In reaching the number 613 Maimonides was careful not to count the same law twice. But this procedure produced an interesting contradiction. For example, the law forbidding boiling a kid in its mother's milk appears first in Exodus 23:19. There the law is given number 92. When the same law appears again in Exodus 34:26, it is counted again as law number 113. When it appears a third time in Deuteronomy 14:21, it is not given a third number.

**THE TRADITION OF 613 LAWS OF THE TORAH
DIVIDED IN ACCORDANCE WITH MODERN
BIBLICAL CRITICISM**

CHART 6b

Genesis	3 laws
Exodus before the Ten Commandments	21 laws
Ten Commandments	14 laws
Covenant Code	54 laws
Remainder of Exodus	22 laws
(includes the Ritual Decalogue)	
Leviticus before the Holiness Code	71 laws
Holiness Code	164 laws
From end of the Holiness Code through Numbers	64 laws
Deuteronomy before the Deuteronomic Code	22 laws
Deuteronomic Code	175 laws
After the Deuteronomic Code	3 laws
	TOTAL 613 laws

Why is the law counted twice? Rabbi Joseph Telushkin explains that Jewish law draws different legal implications for the first two occurrences.[5]

When the Ten Commandments are repeated in Deuteronomy, the laws are not counted a second time, except for the commandment against coveting. The reason for this is because the commandment against coveting has different wording in Deuteronomy. In Exodus 20 the word translated "covet" is *hamod.* In Deuteronomy 5 the word *Lo titaveh* is used and is translated "do not desire." It is also interesting to note that Maimonides extracted fourteen laws from the Ten Commandments of Exodus 20. The fourteen laws are numbered 25 to 38 (see Chart 6c).

At the end of the nineteenth century a well-regarded rabbi of Eastern Europe, Chaffetz Chaim, wrote a book entitled *The Short Book of the Commandments.* Rabbi Chaim pointed out that laws dealing with the temple and the sacrificial system could no longer be obeyed, and he estimated that fewer than 300 of the 613 laws could be considered applicable today.

THE TEN COMMANDMENTS OF EXODUS
SUPPLY FOURTEEN LAWS TO THE
RABBINICAL TRADITION OF 613 LAWS

CHART 6c

Rabbinical Numeration of 613 Laws:	Jewish Numbering of the the Decalogue:
25 Believe in God (I am the LORD your God).	(1)
26 Have no gods before me (Yahweh).	(2)
27 Graven images forbidden.	"
28 You shall not bow down to images or idols.	"
29 You are forbidden to imitate idol worshipers.	"
30 Prohibition against using God's name in vain.	(3)
31 Remember the sabbath day to keep it holy.	(4)
32 Prohibition against working on the sabbath.	"
33 Honor your father and your mother.	(5)
34 You shall not murder.	(6)
35 You shall not commit adultery.	(7)
36 You shall not steal.	(8)
37 You shall not bear false witness.	(9)
38 You shall not covet (neighbor's house or wife).	(10)

Note: (1) When the commandments appear in Exodus 20:1–14, there is no statement that they are ten in number. Later, in Exodus 34:28, the words "ten commandments" appear. (2) When the rabbinical tradition encountered the commandments in Deuteronomy 5, the commandments were not added to the compiled list of 613 because they had already been enumerated from Exodus 20. But the last commandment in Deuteronomy 5 contains a different word for *covet,* and the command "You shall not crave your neighbor's house or his field," became law number 416 of the total 613 Laws. (See also chapter 7 below, "The Decalogues of the Torah.")

The 613 Laws of the Torah in Order

In the listing of the 613 laws that follows, the verse numbers cited are from the Hebrew Bible and frequently differ from English translations.

Genesis

1. Be fruitful and multiply.	1:28
2. Every male among you shall be circumcised.	17:10
3. The thigh muscle on the hip socket of a cooked animal is not to be eaten.	32:33

Exodus

4. The first month of the year shall be this month, Nisan, also called Abib.	12:2
5. On the fourteenth day of the first month the assembly shall slaughter the paschal lamb at twilight.	12:6
6. The slaughtered lamb to be eaten the same night.	12:8
7. The lamb must be roasted, not boiled.	12:8
8. Do not leave any of the lamb until morning.	12:10
9. Remove all leaven from your house for passover.	12:15
10. You must eat unleavened bread during passover.	12:18
11. No leaven shall be found in your house for seven days.	12:19
12. You shall eat nothing leavened during passover.	12:20
13. A foreigner shall not eat the paschal lamb.	12:43
14. A hired servant shall not eat the paschal lamb.	12:45
15. No part of the lamb shall be removed from the house.	12:46
16. No bone of the lamb shall be broken.	12:46
17. No uncircumcised can eat of the paschal lamb.	12:48
18. The firstborn of man and beast is consecrated to God.	13:2
19. No food primarily leavened shall be eaten during passover.	13:3
20. No leaven shall be found in all your territory during passover.	13:7

21. You shall explain to your son the meaning of passover.   13:8
22. Every firstborn donkey you shall redeem with a sheep.   13:13
23. If you don't redeem the firstborn donkey you shall
    break its neck.   13:13
24. Everyone shall stay near home on the seventh day.   16:29
25. The commandment to acknowledge the
    LORD God as the one who delivered Israel from Egypt.   20:2
26. You shall have no gods besides me.   20:3
27. You shall not make for yourself an idol in any form.   20:4
28. You shall not bow down to idols.   20:5
29. You shall not worship idols.   20:5
30. You shall not take the name of the LORD in vain.   20:7
31. Remember the sabbath day to keep it holy.   20:8
32. Prohibition against you or your household working
    on the sabbath day.   20:10
33. Honor your father and mother.   20:12
34. You shall not (kill) murder.   20:13
35. You shall not commit adultery.   20:14
36. You shall not steal.   20:15
37. Do not bear false witness against your neighbor.   20:16
38. Do not covet your neighbor's property or spouse.   20:14
39. You shall not make any gods of silver or of gold.   20:20
40. You shall not make an altar of hewn stones for me.   22:22
41. You shall not ascend by steps to my altar.   20:26
42. A Hebrew slave shall be released after six years.   21:2
43. If a master dislikes a female slave he shall let her
    be redeemed.   21:8
44. Further rights of a female slave.   21:9–11
45. A master cannot resell a female slave.   21:8
46. The three rights of a purchased wife.   21:10
47. Whoever kills with a blow shall be put to death.   21:12
48. Whoever strikes his parents shall be put to death.   21:15
49. Whoever injures with fist or stone is liable.   21:18–19
50. Whoever strikes and kills a slave shall be put to death.   21:20
51. When an ox gores a person to death it must be stoned.   21:28
52. The meat of the stoned ox must not be eaten.   21:28
53. When the above ox was in the habit of goring.   21:29
54. When a man opens a pit and injury occurs.   21:33
55. When a person's livestock grazes another's field.   22:4
56. When a fire damages his neighbor's field.   22:5
57. When an item given for safekeeping is stolen.   22:6
58. When a possession becomes dishonestly appropriated.   22:8

59. When a man is unable to guard an animal given for safekeeping. 22:9–12
60. When a borrowed animal is maimed or dies. 22:13
61. When a man seduces a virgin who is not engaged. 22:16–17
62. You shall not permit a sorcerer to live. 22:18
63. You shall not molest an alien. 22:20
64. You shall not oppress an alien. 22:20
65. You shall not wrong any widow or orphan. 22:21
66. You shall not demand interest for a loan to the poor. 22:24
67. If your needy neighbor's pledge is his cloak, return it before sunset. 22:24–26
68. Do not abuse a needy person by charging interest. 22:24
69. You are prohibited from cursing God. 22:27
70. You are prohibited from cursing a judge. 22:27
71. You shall not curse a prince of your people. 22:27
72. You shall not delay your agricultural offerings. 22:28
73. Flesh mangled in the field you shall not eat. 22:30
74. You shall not spread a false report. 23:1
75. You will not act as an unjust witness. 23:1
76. Do not follow the majority in an unjust act. 23:2
77. You shall not give false testimony in a trial. 23:2
78. You must abide by the majority decision in court. 23:2
79. Do not be partial to the poor in a lawsuit. 23:3
80. You must help enemy's animal when overburdened. 23:5
81. You shall not pervert justice due to your poor. 23:6
82. Do not bring death on the innocent person. 23:7
83. Never take a bribe for a bribe blinds officials. 23:8
84. Let your land lie fallow every seventh year. 23:10–11
85. On the seventh day you and yours shall rest. 23:12
86. Never mention the name of any other god. 23:13
87. It is forbidden to lead Israelites into idolatry. 23:13
88. Three times a year you will hold pilgrimage festivals: passover, weeks, and booths. 23:14–17
89. You will not offer the blood of my sacrifice with leavened bread. 23:18
90. The fat of my offering not to be kept overnight. 23:18
91. First fruits are to be brought to the LORD's house. 23:19
92. You shall not boil a kid in its mother's milk. 23:19
93. Make no covenant with Canaanites or their gods. 23:32
94. Canaanites must not abide in your land. 23:33
95. Israel will make a sanctuary for me in the land. 25:8
96. Poles must always remain in the rings of the ark. 25:15

97.	Shewbread shall always be on a special table.	25:30
98.	A lamp shall be kept burning in the sanctuary.	27:20
99.	The vestments specified for the priests.	28:4–5
100.	Instructions for attaching the breastplate to the ephod.	28:28
101.	The opening of a priest's robe shall have a binding.	28:32
102.	Only the sons of Aaron shall eat the ordination ram.	29:32
103.	When Aaron shall burn incense in front of the veil.	30:7
104.	Offerings are restricted on the altar of gold.	30:3–9
105.	Families shall pay an annual half shekel temple tax.	30:13
106.	Priests to wash their hands and feet when ministering.	30:19–31
107.	The blending of sacred anointing oil.	30:25, 26, 30
108.	Special anointing oil, which shall be sacred.	30:32
109.	Replicating the anointing oil is forbidden.	30:32
110.	Sacred incense not to be replicated for other use.	30:37
111.	You cannot eat a sacrifice to an idol.	34:15
112.	Observe sabbath even at plowing and harvest time.	34:21
113.	You may not eat milk and meat together.	34:26
114.	You shall kindle no fire on the sabbath day.	35:3

Leviticus

115.	Your burnt offering must be without blemish at the tent of meeting.	1:3
116.	Requirements for an offering of meal to the Lord.	2:1–3
117.	Prohibition against a leaven or honey altar offering.	2:11
118.	You shall not omit salt with your grain offerings.	2:13
119.	With all your offerings you shall include salt.	2:13
120.	Offering for a sin committed by the whole people.	4:13–14
121.	If an ordinary person sins unintentionally.	4:27–28
122.	The necessity to testify in the interest of truth.	5:1
123.	When two doves or pigeons can be used as an offering.	5:7
124.	The priest shall not sever the head of a bird offering.	5:8
125.	When fine flour can be accepted as a sin offering.	5:11
126.	An offering of flour shall not contain oil or incense.	5:11
127.	A special penalty for personal use of a sacred item.	5:15
128.	An unintentional sin requires a sin offering when discovered.	5:15–16
129.	A guilt offering required when one deals deceitfully.	5:21
130.	One must restore what is taken by theft or fraud.	5:21–23
131.	The priest shall remove ashes of burnt offerings.	6:3–4
132–3.	Fire on the central altar must never go out.	6:5–6

173.	Reentry procedure for a person with skin disease.	14:2–4
174.	Reentry ritual for a person with skin disease.	14:9
175.	Final ritual for one cured of skin disease.	14:9
176.	The offering required after being cured of above.	14:10–11
177.	When a house is infected by skin disease.	14:35–42
178.	A man with a chronic discharge is unclean.	15:2
179.	Offering for a man cured of a chronic discharge.	15:13–15
180.	A man who has an emission of semen is unclean.	15:16
181.	A menstruating woman is ritually unclean.	15:19
182.	A woman with an irregular discharge is unclean.	15:25
183.	Offering of a woman cured of irregular discharge.	15:28
184.	Aaron not to go behind the curtain for no reason.	16:2–3
185.	Priestly rituals to be performed on Yom Kippur.	16:3–34
186.	Only at the entrance of the tent of meeting can an animal be slaughtered.	17:3–4
187.	The blood of a slain wild animal must be covered.	17:13
188.	You shall not uncover the nakedness of near of kin.	18:6
189.	The nakedness of your father you shall not uncover.	18:7
190.	The nakedness of your mother you shall not uncover.	18:7
191.	Do not uncover the nakedness of your father's wife.	18:7
192.	Do not uncover the nakedness of your sister.	18:9
193.	Do not uncover the nakedness of your granddaughters.	18:10
194.	The above refers to your son's and daughter's daughters.	
195.	Do not uncover the nakedness of your daughter.[6]	
196.	Do not uncover the nakedness of your half sister.	18:11
197.	Do not uncover the nakedness of your father's sister.	18:12
198.	Do not uncover the nakedness of your mother's sister.	18:13
199.	Do not uncover the nakedness of your uncle.[7]	18:14
200.	Do not approach your uncle's wife.	18:14
201.	Do not uncover the nakedness of daughter-in-law.	18:15
202.	Do not uncover the nakedness of your brother's wife.	18:16
203.	Do not uncover the nakedness of a woman and daughter.	18:17
204.	Sex with a woman and her son's daughter is forbidden.	18:17
205.	Sex with a woman and her daughter's daughter is forbidden.	18:17
206.	Do not marry sisters while they are both living.	18:18
207.	Do not approach a woman during her menstruation.	18:19
208.	You shall not sacrifice (immolate) a child to Molech.	18:21
209.	You shall not lie with a male as with a woman.	18:22
210.	You (male) shall not have sex with an animal.	18:23
211.	You (female) shall not have sex with an animal.	18:23
212.	You shall each revere your mother and father.	19:3
213.	Do not turn to idol worship.	19:4

214.	Do not make or cast images for yourself.	19:4
215.	Peace offering not eaten by third day must be burned.	19:6
216.	Do not reap your harvest to the edge of your fields.	19:9
217.	At harvest leave fruit and grain for the poor.	19:10
218.	Do not gather the gleanings of your harvest.	19:9–10
219.	Leave the gleanings of your harvest for the poor.	19:10
220.	You shall not pick your vineyard bare.	19:10
221.	Leave some vineyard fruit for the poor and strangers.	19:10
222.	Do not gather the fallen fruit of your vineyard.	19:10
223.	Leave fallen fruit for the poor and strangers.	19:10
224.	You shall not steal.[8]	19:11
225.	You shall not lie or deal falsely with each other.	19:11
226.	You shall not swear falsely.	19:12
227.	You shall not swear falsely by my (God's) name.	19:12
228.	You shall not defraud your fellow.	19:13
229.	You shall not rob (using force) your fellow.	19:13
230.	Do not hold the wages of a day laborer overnight.	19:13
231.	You shall not curse the deaf.	19:14
232.	Do not put a stumbling block in front of the blind.	19:14
233.	Do not act dishonestly in rendering justice.	19:15
234.	Do not show partiality to the weak.	19:15
235.	Do not show deference to the rich or mighty.	19:15
236.	You shall not go about as a slanderer.	19:16
237.	Do not stand by while your neighbor's blood is shed.	19:16
238.	Do not hate your brother in your heart.	19:17
239.	Reprove your brother when necessary.	19:17
240.	In reproving your brother do not sin.	19:17
241.	You shall not take revenge against your neighbor.	19:18
242.	You shall not bear a grudge against your neighbor.	19:18
243.	You shall love your neighbor as yourself.	19:18
244.	Do not breed an animal with a different species.	19:19
245.	Do not sow a field with two different kinds of seed.	19:19
246.	Do not eat fruit of a new tree for three years.	19:23
247.	A tree's fruit of the fourth year is sacred to God.	19:24
248.	You shall not eat anything with its blood.	19:26
249.	Do not practice divination.	19:26
250.	Do not practice soothsaying.	19:26
251.	Do not cut your hair at the temples.	19:27
252.	Do not trim the edges of your beard.	19:27
253.	Do not tattoo yourselves.	19:28
254.	Reverence my sanctuary; I am the LORD.	19:30
255.	Do not turn to mediums.	19:31

256.	Do not consult wizards (fortunetellers).	19:31
257.	You shall respect and defer before the old.	19:32
258.	Do not cheat in measuring length, weight, or quantity.	19:35
259.	You shall have honest weights and balances.	19:36
260.	All who curse father and mother shall be put to death.	20:9
261.	If a man shall take mother and daughter he shall die.	20:14
262.	Do not follow the practices of the driven-out nation.	20:23
263.	Priests may defile themselves for death of close kin.	21:2
264.	Priest may defile himself for death of virgin sister.	21:3
265.	Priests shall be holy to God to offer in the temple.	21:6
266.	Priests may not marry a prostitute.	21:7
267.	Priests may not marry a defiled woman.	21:7
268.	Priests may not marry a divorced woman.	21:7
269.	You must treat a priest as sacred.	21:8
270.	A high priest cannot come near a dead person.	21:11
271.	The above law includes a dead parent.	21:11
272.	A high priest can only marry a virgin.	21:13
273.	A high priest may not marry a widow.	21:14
274.	A high priest may not have relations with a widow.	21:14
275.	A priest can have no blemish or physical defect.	21:17
276.	Details concerning the above law are provided.	21:18–20
277.	Temple areas where a blemished priest cannot enter.	21:23
278.	An unclean priest cannot eat of a sacred donation.	22:2
279.	A priest with a discharge may not eat sacred donations.	22:4
280.	A layperson may not eat of a sacred donation.	22:10
281.	Servant of a priest may not eat of a sacred donation.	22:10
282.	An uncircumcised priest may not eat of a sacred donation.[9]	
283.	A priest's daughter married to a layman may not eat of a sacred donation.	22:12
284.	No one may eat from produce for an offering.	22:15
285.	A defective animal is not an acceptable offering.	22:20
286.	An acceptable animal for offering must be perfect.	22:20
287.	An animal for offering cannot develop a defect.	22:21
288.	A disabled animal cannot be an offering to the Lord.	22:22
289.	An animal with a discharge cannot be an offering.	22:22
290.	Do not burn a defective animal as an offering.	22:22
291.	Do not offer an animal with injured testicles.	22:24
292.	Do not accept defective offerings from foreigners.	22:25
293.	An offered animal must be at least eight days old.	22:27
294.	Do not sacrifice the same day a beast and its young.	22:28
295.	Do not profane my holy name.	22:32
296.	Sanctify my holy name.	22:32

297. The first day of passover is a sacred occasion.   23:7
298. You shall do no work on the first day of passover.   23:7
299. For seven days you shall offer a passover oblation.   23:8
300. The seventh day of passover is a sacred occasion.   23:8
301. Do no work on the seventh day of passover.   23:8
302. Bring a wave offering of your first fruits.   23:10–11
303. Cereal grain must be offered before it is eaten.   23:14
304. Parched grain must be offered before it is eaten.   23:14
305. Fresh ears must be offered before they are eaten.   23:14
306. When to start counting seven weeks to pentecost.   23:15
307. On the first day of weeks offer two loaves of bread.   23:16
308. On the first day of pentecost you shall not work.   23:21
309. The first day of pentecost (weeks) is a sacred day.   23:21
310. On the first day of the seventh month do not work.   23:24–25
311. The above day is a sacred day, Rosh ha-Shana.   23:24–25
312. On the above day offer an oblation to the LORD.   23:25
313. The tenth day of the seventh month is the day of
      atonement (Yom Kippur)   23:27
314. On Yom Kippur bring an offering by fire to God.   23:27
315. The tenth day of the seventh month is Yom Kippur.   23:28
316. You will do no work on Yom Kippur.   23:28
317. You must practice self-denial during Yom Kippur.   23:29
318. The fifteenth day, seventh month is the feast of booths. 23:34
319. The first day of booths is sacred. Do no work.   23:35
320. Offer an oblation for the seven days of booths.   23:36
321. The eighth day of booths is a sacred occasion.   23:36
322. Offer a special oblation on the eighth day of booths.   23:36
323. On the eighth day of booths you shall do no work.   23:36
324. On the first day of booths gather special branches.   23:40
325. You shall dwell in booths for the seven days.   23:42
326. Do not work your land during the seventh year.   25:4
327. On the seventh year the land shall have complete rest.   25:4
328. Do not harvest the aftergrowth in the seventh year.   25:5
329. Do not systemically pick fruit the seventh year.   25:5
330. How to determine the year of jubilee.   25:8
331. Sound a ram's horn to announce the year of jubilee.   25:9
332. You shall hallow the fiftieth year.   25:10
333. During jubilee you will not sow the land.   25:11
334. During jubilee you will not reap or harvest the land.   25:11
335. You may only eat from your vines directly.   25:12
336. When you sell land you shall not cheat your neighbor.   25:14
337. When you buy land you shall not cheat your neighbor.   25:14

338. You will not cheat one another.   25:17
339. Land shall not be sold in perpetuity.   25:23
340. You shall provide for the redemption of the land.   25:24
341. When a house within a walled city is sold.   25:29
342. Open land of the Levites may not be sold.   25:34
343. Support your kin and do not take interest from them.   25:37
344. Fellow Israelites are not to be treated as slaves.   25:42
345. Whom I delivered from Egypt are not to be as slaves.   25:42
346. You shall not treat Hebrew slaves with harshness.   25:43
347. No Israelite may be passed on as a perpetual slave.   25:46
348. Israelite debt slaves may be redeemed from aliens.   25:53
349. Do not erect an idol or stone figure for worship.   26:1
350. The value of persons for whom offerings are paid.   27:1–7
351. If offering an animal do not substitute good for bad.   27:10
352. If offering an animal do not substitute bad for good.   27:10
353. Priest will set the value of an unclean animal offering.   27:12
354. Priest will set the value of a house as an offering.   27:14
355. Determining the redemption value of a vowed field.   27:16
356. No one shall vow a firstborn animal to the LORD.[10]   27:26
357–59. Special rules for the fate of persons or things
          vowed to Yahweh.   27:28
360. How to determine the tithe of the LORD from the herd.   27:32
361. Do not exchange a good animal for a bad for the tithe.   27:32

Numbers

362. Unclean Israelites must be put outside the camp.   5:23
363. Unclean Israelites must not defile the sanctuary.   5:23
364. A person who wrongs one must confess and make amends.   5:6–7
365. Procedures taken against a suspected adulteress.   5:12–15
366. A jealous husband must take his wife to the priests.   5:15
367. A suspected wife to be accompanied by a meal offering.   5:15
368. When a person utters a Nazirite vow.   6:2
369. A Nazirite shall abstain from wine and strong drink.   6:3
370. A Nazirite must not drink anything steeped in grapes.   6:3
371. A Nazirite shall not eat grape skins or seeds.   6:3
372. A Nazirite shall not eat dried grapes from a vine.   6:4
373. A razor shall not touch a Nazirite's hair.   6:5
374. A Nazirite must let his hair grow freely.   6:5
375. A Nazirite must not enter where a dead person is.   6:6–7
376. A Nazirite cannot touch his kin when the kin dies.   6:6–7

Deuteronomy

416. Do not crave (desire) your neighbor's house or field.   5:21
417. Hear, O Israel, the LORD is our God, the LORD alone.   6:4
418. You shall love the LORD your God.   6:5
419. Diligently teach the Torah to your children.   6:7
420. Speak of and study Torah wherever you are day and night.   6:7
421. Bind the laws as a sign on your arm.   6:8
422. Let the laws be as a pendant on your forehead.   6:8
423. Write the laws on the doorposts of your houses.   6:9
424. Do not put the LORD your God to a test.   6:16
425. Destroy the seven nations that you will displace.   7:2
426. Show no mercy to these idol worshipers.   7:2
427. Prohibit your children from marrying those driven out.   7:3
428. Do not become ensnared by the silver and gold of idols.   7:25
429. Do not bring an abominable thing into your house.   7:26
430. You must bless the LORD after meals.   8:10
431. You must befriend the alien, as you were once aliens.   10:19
432. Fear God and hold fast to him.   10:20
433. Only the LORD shall you serve.   10:20
434. Only the LORD shall you worship.   10:20
435. Only in the LORD's name shall you swear.   10:20
436. Destroy the places where the nations worshiped.   12:2
437. Worship God only in the place and way that he chooses.   12:4
438. At God's chosen place rejoice and bring offerings.   12:5–6
439. Take care not to make offerings in just any place.   12:13
440. Only worship in the place that the LORD shall choose.   12:13
441. In your communities you may slaughter and eat meat.   12:15
442–49. Eight prohibitions concerning eating, related to
    tithes and offerings.   12:17–18
450. Take care that you do not neglect the Levite.   12:19
451. When you may slaughter and eat of your herd.   12:21
452. You shall not eat the life with the meat.   12:23
453. Bring votive offerings and gifts to the chosen place.   12:26
454. Be careful not to add to the laws that I enjoin on you.   13:1
455. Do not subtract from the laws that I enjoin on you.   13:1
456. Ignore prophets who lead you to worship another god.   13:2–4
457–462. Six laws demanding the execution of those
    who would entice my people to worship other
    gods or idols.   13:6–14
463. In the above, judges must investigate thoroughly.   13:15
464. You shall destroy the city that worships other gods.   13:16
465. That city (above) is doomed and can never be rebuilt.   13:17
466. You shall retain nothing from the destroyed city.   13:18

512. One who casts spells is forbidden.   18:11
513. Consulting a medium is forbidden.   18:11
514. Consulting a wizard is forbidden.   18:11
515. Making enquiries from the dead is forbidden.   18:11
516. To a true prophet from your kinsmen you shall listen.   18:15
517. One who speaks in the names of other gods shall die.   18:20
518. Speaking falsely in God's name is a capital offense.   18:20
519. Do not fear a false prophet or the words of a false prophet. 18:22
520. Establish three cities of refuge in your land.   19:2–3
521. Have no pity on a vicious murderer.   19:11
522. Do not move your neighbor's boundary marker.   19:14
523. Two witnesses are needed to sustain a conviction.   19:15
524. How to determine the punishment of a false witness.   19:18
525. Do not fear superior forces when the LORD is with you.   20:1
526. The priest shall speak to the troops before battle.   20:2
527. A law containing four exemptions from army service.   20:5–9
528. Before destroying a town in war offer terms of peace.   20:10
529. Do not destroy fruit-bearing trees of a besieged town.   20:19
530. When a murdered person is found in open country.   21:1–8
531. The law of the heifer and the wadi of running water.   21:4
532. A captured woman is entitled to mourn before marriage.   21:13
533. A captured woman shall not be sold as a slave.   21:14
534. If you are not satisfied with her (above) set her free.   21:14
535. You must execute a person guilty of a capital offense.   21:22
536. Do not allow an executed convict to hang overnight.   21:22
537. You must bury an executed convict on the day of death.   21:23
538. Do not ignore a neighbor's ox that wanders away.   22:1
539. You must return your neighbor's lost property.   22:1
540. You shall not ignore your neighbor's fallen beast.   22:4
541. You must help your neighbor raise his fallen beast.   22:4
542. A woman shall not wear a man's apparel.   22:5
543. A man shall not wear a woman's apparel.   22:5
544. You shall not take a nesting bird with her eggs.   22:6
545. You may take the eggs but the nesting bird goes free.   22:6
546. When you build a house put a guardrail on your roof.   22:8
547. If someone falls off your roof, you are guilty.   22:8
548. Do not sow your vineyard with two kinds of seeds.   22:9
549. If you do (above) your produce must be forfeited.   22:9
550. You shall not plow with an ox and donkey together.   22:10
551. You shall not wear woven cloth of wool and linen.   22:11
552. A man should marry a woman before living with her.[12]   22:13

553–54.	A falsely accused wife can insist on remaining the man's wife. He cannot divorce her.	22:13–19
555.	Two adulterers are to be stoned in the gate.	22:24
556.	A man who rapes a woman in a field shall be stoned.	22:26
557.	A man who deflowers an unengaged woman must marry her.	22:28
558.	The man (above) pays a *mohar* and may not divorce her.	22:29
559.	A sexually mutilated man may not enter the community.	23:2
560.	A bastard child is not to be admitted to the community.	23:3
561.	Ammonites and Moabites cannot become Israelites.	23:4–6
562.	Do not promote the peace of Moabites or Ammonites.	23:7
563.	Do not abhor the Edomite or the Egyptian.	23:8
564.	Edomites and Egyptians may become citizens in time.	23:9
565.	An unclean man must become clean to reenter the camp.	23:11
566.	Soldiers in camp must cover their excrement carefully.	23:14
567.	Soldiers must keep a trowel to keep a sanitary camp.	23:14
568.	Do not return a slave who takes refuge with you.	23:16
569.	Allow the slave (above) to live in the community.	23:17
570.	An Israelite man or woman cannot be a prostitute.[13]	23:18
571.	Do not offer God a prostitute's fee or wages of a dog [male prostitute].	23:19
572.	Do not demand interest from an Israelite on anything.	23:20
573.	You may demand interest from a foreigner.	23:21
574.	Do not delay in fulling a vow to the LORD.	23:22
575.	You must keep your promises and your vows to God.	23:24
576.	Eat grapes of a vineyard but do not fill a basket.	23:25
577.	Pluck ears as you pass your neighbor's field.	23:25
578.	But do not put a sickle to your neighbor's grain.	23:25
579.	A divorced wife must receive a written bill of divorce.	24:1
580.	When a man cannot remarry his divorced wife.	24:2–4
581.	A newly married man is exempt from military service.	24:5
582.	The exemption (above) shall be for one year.	24:6
583.	It is unjust to take a hand mill as a pledge.	24:6
584.	Kidnapping for enslavement is a capital crime.	24:7
585.	Do not enter a man's house to seize his pledge.	24:10
586.	Do not sleep in a garment used as a pledge.	24:12
587.	Return a sleeping garment if it is needed.	24:13
588.	Pay laborers the same day that they work.	24:15–16
589.	Fathers are not guilty for children and vice versa.	24:16
590.	Do not mistreat an alien or orphan.	24:17
591.	You shall not take a widow's garment in pledge.	24:17
592.	When you reap your field leave a sheaf for the poor.	24:19
593.	The sheaf left behind is for a widow, alien, orphan.	24:19

594. If a criminal receives stripes a judge shall oversee.   25:2
595. A criminal may not receive more than forty stripes.   25:3
596. Do not muzzle an animal while it is threshing.   25:4
597. A man should marry his brother's widow if childless.   25:5
598. The firstborn son (above) shall continue the line
     of the deceased brother.   25:6
599. Procedure if brother-in-law refuses to marry the widow.   25:7
600. A woman not to grab a man's genitals during a fight.   25:11
601. Woman breaking the above law to be severely punished.   25:11
602. You shall not own dishonest weights or measures.   25:13–16
603. Remember what evil Amalak did after you left Egypt.   25:17
604. You shall blot out the memory of Amalak on earth.   25:19
605. Do not forget the above concerning Amalak.   25:19
606. A creedal prayer to say when presenting your first
     fruits to the priest beginning "My father was
     a wandering Aramean."   26:1–10
607. A declaration required with the third-year tithe.   26:12–15
608. A prohibition against eating a tithe while mourning.   26:14
609. A prohibition against eating a tithe while unclean.   26:14
610. A prohibition against offering a tithe to the dead.   26:14
611. Israel is commanded to walk in God's ways.   28:9
612. The law to be read every seventh year at booths.   31:10
613. Write down this song and teach it to all Israel.[14]   31:19

7

The Decalogues of the Torah

Then God spoke all these words. (Exod 20:1)

In this chapter we will briefly discuss the Ten Commandments, found in both Exodus 20 and Deuteronomy 5, and a less familiar short collection of commands found in Exodus 34. Since the days of Wellhausen the familiar version of the commandments (Exodus 20 and Deuteronomy 5) has been referred to as the *Ethical* Decalogue, and the commandments of Exodus 34 as the *Ritual* Decalogue.

The Ethical Decalogue (Exodus 20 and Deuteronomy 5) is attributed originally to the E source, and the less familiar Ritual Decalogue (Exodus 34) is attributed to the J source. But all three (Exodus 20, Exodus 34, and Deuteronomy 5) display ample evidence of additional scribal editorial activity.

Exodus 20:1–17

These verses constitute the most widely known passage of the Hebrew Bible. It is interesting to note that the passage, along with the chapters that appear before and after, contain no mention of "ten commandments" and no mention of tablets of stone. The phrase "tablets of stone" does not appear until Exodus 24:12, after the Covenant Code. The number ten is applied to the number of laws received by Moses from God for the first time in Exodus 34:28, where it seems to refer to the Ritual Decalogue rather than the more familiar Ethical Decalogue of Exodus 20.

THE TEN COMMANDMENTS OF EXODUS 20

CHART 7a

Jewish Division of the Ethical Decalogue:

1. Believe in God (I am the LORD your God).[1]
2. Have no other gods before me (Yahweh).
   Graven images forbidden.
   You shall not bow down to images or idols.
3. Prohibition against using God's name in vain.
4. Remember the sabbath day to keep it holy.
5. Honor your father and your mother.
6. You shall not murder.
7. You shall not commit adultery.
8. You shall not steal.
9. You shall not bear false witness.
10. You shall not covet (neighbor's house or wife, etc).

Facts Concerning the Ethical Decalogue of Exodus 20

We have already mentioned that there is no indication as to the number of commandments as they are recorded in Exodus 20 and that there is no mention of the commands being written on tablets of stone or anything else. We read only that "God spoke all these words" (20:1). There are other facts to note: (a) All commands are directed to the second-person singular. (b) The first two commands are in the first person, with God as the speaker (see chart 7a); in the next three commands (name/sabbath/father and mother) God is spoken of in the third person. (c) All these commands are unconditional. They are apodictic. There are no casuistic laws in the collection. (d) There are only two positive commands ("Honor your father and mother," and "Remember the sabbath day"). (e) There are no penalties or sanctions for breaking the commands, although the command to honor father and mother carries with it the promise that your days may be long in the land. (f) Although this summary of basic commands has been placed in this location in Exodus by the priestly author known as P, there is no mention of priestly concerns such as animal sacrifices, temple activity, or dietary laws. (g) Two of these commands are related to speech (wrongfully using Yahweh's name and bearing false witness).

The opening laws are about the individual's relation to Yahweh, and the laws that follow the sabbath command have to do with human relationships. In other words, religious laws are followed by social laws. As to why no punishments are linked to these commands, the thought has been advanced that these commands are meant to serve as a summary of goals for all individuals who make up Yahweh's people and are not laws in the traditional sense. Punishments mentioned here would be inappropriate.[2] Elsewhere in the Pentateuch most of these laws are associated with severe punishments. For example, in Leviticus we read:

> One who blasphemes the name of the LORD shall be put to death. (Lev 24:16)

> Anyone who kills a human being shall be put to death. (Lev 24:17)

The Same Commandments in Deuteronomy 5

The commands of Exodus 20 appear in Deuteronomy 5, where they are called the Ten Commandments (Deut 4:13).[3] While the Ten Commandments of Deuteronomy are primarily the same as Exodus 20, there are interesting differences (see Chart 7b).

The Motivational Clause for Keeping the Sabbath

The reason for keeping the sabbath in Exodus 20 was an editorial addition of a priestly redactor. The reference to the creation of the world in six days with God resting on the seventh day supported the priestly account of creation as it appears in Genesis 1. In Genesis 1 Elohim is boxed in by a seven-day week. It can be argued that the Aaronid priests in Babylonian exile used their powerful creation account to promote their theological goals. In order to promote and preserve the strengthening of Judahite identity in captivity the priests insisted on the keeping of the weekly sabbath. In a brilliant fashion the scribes of the Aaronids built the sacredness of the sabbath into the creation activity of God.[4]

When the sabbath command appears in Deuteronomy, a different reason is given for keeping the sabbath.

> Remember that you were a slave in the land of Egypt, and the LORD your God brought you out from there with a mighty hand and an outstretched arm;[5] therefore the LORD your God commanded you to keep the sabbath day. (Deut 5:15)

In the Deuteronomic explanation for keeping the sabbath there is no mention of creation. The observance of the sabbath is for the benefit of

DIFFERENCES BETWEEN THE TEN COMMANDMENTS OF EXODUS 20 AND THOSE OF DEUTERONOMY 5

CHART 7b

1. A typical Deuteronomic expression, "that it may go well with you," is added to the command to honor your father and mother.

2. In Exodus the opening word of the sabbath command is "remember" *(zakor).* In Deuteronomy it is "observe" *(samor).*

3. In the Deuteronomy version of the sabbath command (Deut 5:12) these words are added: "as the LORD your God commanded you."

4. The motivational clause supporting the sabbath command in Deuteronomy is completely different from the Exodus explanation. There is no mention in Deuteronomy of God creating the world in six days and resting on the seventh.

5. In the law forbidding coveting, the neighbor's wife is removed from the list of the neighbor's property and appears in a separate sentence (Deut 5:21a).

6. In Deuteronomy another word besides "covet" *(hamod)* is used. The word "crave" or "desire" is also used *(avah).*

workers. Children and household slaves, donkeys and livestock, and even resident aliens deserve a day of rest. You are to remember that your ancestors were once slave laborers in Egypt.

The fact that two redactors felt free to add motivational clauses to this sabbath command is informative in itself. It demonstrates that scribes did not hesitate to add additional wording to this collection. The original sabbath command was short and raises the possibility that all the original Ten Commandments were brief to promote memorization. For example, the original commandments probably did not contain the following paragraph:

> For I the LORD your God am a jealous God, punishing children for the iniquity of their parents, to the third and fourth generation of those who reject me, but showing steadfast love to the thousandth generation of those who love me and keep my commandments. (Deut 5:9)

Since it is obvious that the popular form of the Ten Commandments (Exodus 20 and Deuteronomy 5) has been emended, scholars believe that what we have is the end product of a period of developmental growth. The original set was made up of brief, metrical statements, but this has been obscured by scribal editing to make the commandments adhere to a more complex theological perspective; in the case of the sabbath command two different theological perspectives are evident.[6]

Because the Ethical Decalogue of Exodus 20 is encountered first by a reader of the canonical Torah, many Bible readers assume that Exodus 20 predates Deuteronomy 5. This may not be the case. Some scholars believe that Exodus 20 is a modified copy of Deuteronomy 5, and that Deuteronomy 5 was influenced by the tablet tradition of Exodus 34. (See Exod 34:1 and 28, also Deut 5:22.)[7]

The Ritual Decalogue (Exodus 34:10–28)

> He [God] said: I hereby make a covenant....And he [Moses] wrote on the tablets the words of the covenant, the ten commandments.[8] (Exod 34:10, 28)

Chapter 34 of Exodus has been identified as one of the most difficult portions of Exodus to understand.[9] The annual festivals are listed and are similar to the festivals of the Covenant Code. But the festivals are not listed together; they are separated by text concerning the firstborn (vv. 19f.) and the sabbath (v. 21). Like Part II of the Book of the Covenant, where apodictic laws predominate, God is sometimes the speaker (vv. 11, 18, 19, 20, 24, 25), but other verses speak of God in the third person (14, 23, 24b, 26a). Also, while the opening phrases place a distance between the Israelites and the people of the land who will be driven out, verse 15 suggests that they are neighbors:

> For when they prostitute themselves to their gods and sacrifice to their gods, someone among them will invite you, and you will eat of the sacrifice. (Exod 34:15)

It seems as if Moses is producing a second set of tablets to replace the tablets he broke when he came down the mountain and saw the people dancing around the golden calf that Aaron had made:

> Moses' anger burned hot, and he threw the tablets from his hands and broke them at the foot of the mountain. (Exod 32:19).

LAWS OF THE RITUAL DECALOGUE (EXODUS 34)

CHART 7c

- Do not make a covenant with the inhabitants of the land.

- Tear down their altars, break their pillars, and cut down their sacred poles.

- You shall not make cast idols.

- You shall keep the festival of unleavened bread.

- All that first opens the womb is mine.

- The firstborn donkey shall be redeemed with a lamb.

- No one shall appear before me empty-handed.

- Six days you shall work, but on the seventh day you shall rest.

- You shall observe the festival of weeks, the first fruits of wheat harvest.

- [You shall observe] the festival of ingathering at the turn of the year.

- You shall not offer the blood of my sacrifice with leaven.

- The sacrifice of the festival of passover shall not be left until the morning.

- The best of the first fruits of your ground you shall bring to the house of the LORD your God.

- You shall not boil a kid in its mother's milk.

There are fourteen laws listed above. If we combine the requirement of the three annual pilgrimage festivals into one, there will be twelve commands. In order to reach the number ten referred to in Exodus 34:28 we have to assume that several commands were added to the original listing by a redactor, which is quite common in the Hebrew Bible.

The original tablets had been written by the finger of God.

> When God finished speaking with Moses on Mount Sinai, he gave him
> the two tablets of the covenant, tablets of stone, written with the finger
> of God. (Exod 31:18)

But in Exodus 34 we read:

> The LORD said to Moses: Write these words…and he [Moses] wrote on
> the tablets the words of the covenant, the ten commandments. (Exod
> 34:27–28)

Because there are levels of authorship in Exodus 34, it may very well have
been that in an original, shorter account of the incident God was the subject
of verse 28 (the one who wrote on the tablets a second time), not Moses.

While the point can be made that the earlier commandments of Exodus 20 constitute a spiritual summary of the law, beginning with basic obliga-
tions of humans toward God and concluding with the relationships of
humans with each other (religious laws first, followed by social laws), the
same can hardly be said about the laws of Exodus 34. Several of the laws
could hardly be called basic. Two examples are the need to redeem a firstborn donkey and the Canaanite law concerning the restriction on boiling a
kid in its mother's milk.

Many scholars attribute this collection to J.[10] It must be obvious, however, that a Deuteronomic scribe is responsible for the following:[11]

> You shall tear down their altars, break their pillars, and cut down their
> sacred poles. (Exod 34:13)

The Decalogues Taken Together

We observe that the Ethical Decalogue is not typical of the Torah laws
because there is no specific reference to animal sacrifices, offerings, temple
activity, annual festivals, or dietary restrictions. When we look at the Ritual
Decalogue of Exodus 34 we find that this collection serves as a more varied
sample of the variety of biblical law. The Deuteronomic laws to smash their
pillars and cut down or burn their sacred poles appear in the Ritual Decalogue after a command warning against making a covenant with the inhabitants of the land. Then the three annual pilgrimage festivals are mentioned,
opening the area of animal sacrifices, offerings, and dietary requirements.

The reason for the popularity of the Ethical Decalogue in comparison
to the Ritual Decalogue is its universal nature, although the opening statement—"I am the LORD your God who brought you out of the land of Egypt"

(Exod 20:2)—requires that the reader tie these commands to a historical event and marks the commands for an idealized concept presented as historical Israel.

Both summaries (the Ethical Decalogue and the Ritual Decalogue) have their merits and actually complement each other as concrete statements of Yahwism. For this reason we suggest that taken together they serve as a valuable summary of biblical law.

Index to the Decalogues of the Torah (Exodus 20, Deuteronomy 5, Exodus 34)

TC = Ten Commandments/Ethical Decalogue
RD = Ritual Decalogue

Firstborn of male livestock shall be redeemed	Exod 34:19 RD
Firstborn of your sons shall be redeemed	Exod 34:20 RD
Firstborn donkey shall be redeemed with a lamb	Exod 34:20 RD
Gods before me, You shall have no other	Exod 20:3 TC
Gods before me, You shall have no other	Deut 5:7 TC
Idols of anything on land or sea are forbidden	Exod 20:4 TC
Idols of anything on land or sea are forbidden	Deut 5:8 TC
Idols, You shall not make cast	Exod 34:17 RD
Idols: You shall not bow down to them or worship	Exod 20:5 TC
Idols: You shall not bow down to them or worship	Deut 5:9 TC
Leaven, Do not offer the blood of sacrifice with	Exod 34:25 RD
Mother's milk, You shall not boil a kid in its	Exod 34:26 RD
Murder, You shall not	Deut 5:17 TC
Murder, You shall not	Exod 20:13 TC
Name: You shall not misuse God's name	Deut 5:11 TC
Name: You shall not misuse God's name	Exod 20:7 TC
Passover sacrifice not to be left until morning	Exod 34:25 RD
Sabbath day: Observe it and keep it holy	Deut 5:12–15 TC
Sabbath day: You shall keep it holy	Exod 20:8–11 TC
Seventh day, You shall rest on the	Exod 34:21 RD
Steal, You shall not	Exod 20:15 TC
Steal, You shall not	Deut 5:19 TC
Tear down the altars of the people of the land	Exod 34:13 RD
Womb is mine, All that first opens the	Exod 34:19 RD
Worship no other god, You shall	Exod 34:14 RD

8

The Administration of Justice in Ancient Israel

Although there are many scattered references to the administration of justice in the Hebrew Bible, the problem in abstracting a concise picture of legal procedures is increased by the long period of the history of Israel/Judah covered and the ever-present fragmentation of Israel, premonarchical, united monarchical, divided monarchical, urban/rural, exilic, post-exilic.

The problem would be simplified if we could say with authority that a given passage referring to justice administration could be assigned to a specific time period.

Administration of Justice in Premonarchical Israel

The hero stories that comprise the book of Judges do not give us much insight into issues of law and administration in premonarchical Israel, but there is a passage in Judges that is interesting. In Judges 10:1–5, and continuing in chapter 12:7–15, there is a list of judges. This list only contains the name of one of the heros whose stories make up the rest of the book of Judges. Could this list have as its basis the names of men who were judges in the traditional sense of the word?

Regardless, in premonarchical Israel there was no centralization, and if there were judges in the traditional meaning of the word they served only in regional areas. We have a report in 1 Samuel that Samuel himself was a judge and had a circuit consisting of Bethel, Gilgal, Mizpah, and Ramah (1 Sam 7:15–17).

Our best chance of reconstructing the administration of justice in early Israel lies in the area of sociology. If we assume that Israel emerged in the highlands of Canaan at the end of the thirteenth century B.C.E. as a nation of subsistence farmers, we can speculate on the development of legal mores and folkways. The basic institution was the extended family of agriculture, three or four generations living in one location with responsibilities for all age groups. Conflicts within this basic group were settled by the father or a person who served as a father figure.

It is assumed that there were alliances of these families to enhance survival, alliances that enabled families to share resources, responsibilities, and risks. These alliances were called clans *(mishpahoth)*. Conflicts among families making up the clan could be settled by agreements among the family heads.

Justice in the Gate

Although there were no cities early on, towns began to appear as time passed. When these towns grew and walls were constructed around them, a new phase of legal justice was introduced, justice at the gate. The gate was similar to the plaza of Spain and Latin cities of the Americas, an open place for public use and marketing, and a meeting place for social purposes. At the gate elders of the town would meet to discuss and decide matters of public interest. At some point elders with reputations for wisdom and judgment were called upon to restore balance in the community by making legal decisions based on the folkways and the mores of the community.

And so was born the Israelite legal assembly.[1] Nowhere in the Bible do we have the specific details concerning the facts of the legal assembly. There are some questions for which we would like to have answers. Was it necessary to have ten elders? In Ruth 4, Boaz gets ten elders to participate in a legal assembly, but the author of Ruth tells us he is writing in a time long past the lifetime of Boaz (Ruth 4:7). Was there an age limit to be recognized as an elder? After a decision was made by the elders in the gate was there an opportunity for an appeal to another court? Could a number of assemblies be held on the same day, and were there days when it was not proper to hold an assembly?[2]

An appeal to another decision-making body (or decision-maker) may have been possible in some places and in some time periods. Israel was a geographically fragmented country, and there is no reason to expect total conformity of practice in all areas.[3]

Justice at the gate survived for Israel and became a permanent, functional form of legal proceeding. We have many references to it. In the Deuteronomic Code when the brother-in-law of a widow refuses his levirate duty the widow is instructed to go to the elders at the gate.

> The elders of the town shall summon him [the brother-in-law] and speak to him. (Deut 25:8)

The parents of a rebellious son are instructed as follows:

> His father and his mother shall take hold of him and bring him out to
> the elders of his town at the gate. (Deut 21:19)

The prophet Amos is reported to have said:

> Hate evil and love good,
> and establish justice in the gate. (Amos 5:15)

The Tradition of Moses and Justice Administration

Another legal tradition is introduced to us in a familiar passage in Exodus in which advice is given by Jethro to Moses when Moses is said to have
sat as judge for the children of Israel from morning to evening:

> When they [the people] have a dispute they come to me and I decide
> between one person and another, and I make known to them the
> statutes and instructions of God. (Exod 19:16)

Jethro advised Moses to select trustworthy judges, set them as officials over
thousands, hundreds, fifties, and tens, and allow them to settle minor legal
disputes and only bring important cases to Moses. The first problem with
this passage is that it is out of place in the weighty, theological book of Exodus. We assume that it was inserted in the Exodus account to validate legal
procedural decisions made at some time in Israel's history but where, when,
and under what circumstances may not be possible to determine.[4] The concept of dividing the population into thousands, hundreds, and so forth has
been related to military organization.[5]

Martin Noth states that this division for justice administration was
probably the practice in Israel at one time.[6] While he does not identify the
period, he does suggest that the tradition of Jethro's advice may have arisen
at an early period. A second possible time period was the reign of
Jehoshaphat. There is a report in 2 Chronicles that Jehoshaphat appointed
judges in the land and the fortified cities of Judah. He instructed them:

> Take care what you do, for there is no perversion of justice with the
> LORD our God, or partiality, or taking of bribes. (2 Chr 19:7)

The account goes on to say that Jehoshaphat also "appointed certain Levites
and priests…to give judgment…and to decide disputed cases" (2 Chr 19:8).[7]
This has frequently been interpreted as the founding of a supreme court in
Jerusalem. A third possible time period for the division of judges with a possible referral to a Moses figure for decisions in difficult cases is the reign of

Josiah. Since the goal of the Deuteronomists was centralization, they would be interested in a supreme centralized judge or court. Indeed in Deuteronomy we find this concept:

> If a judicial decision is too difficult for you to make between one kind of bloodshed and another, one kind of legal right and another, or one kind of assault and another...then you shall immediately go up to the place which the LORD your God will choose, where you shall consult with the levitical priests and the judge who is in office in those days. (Deut 17:8–9)

Deuteronomy goes on to warn those who make an appeal to the central court that they must accept the decision of the court without exception, under penalty of death (Deut 17:10–13).

The Bribe That Perverts Justice

Interestingly, we learn something of law administration from the frequent mention of the bribe *(kopher)*. First in the Book of the Covenant we read:

> You shall take no bribe, for a bribe blinds the officials, and subverts the cause of those who are in the right. (Exod 23:8)

Notice that there is no punishment specified here for taking a bribe (or elsewhere either), but the reason given for not taking a bribe is that it clouds the reasoning power of those who must make a legal decision.

In Deuteronomy this same law is repeated, specifically condemning the bribe (Deut 16:19), and in an interesting hortatory passage God is praised as one who "takes no bribe" (Deut 10:17).

In three of the four eighth-century prophets there are condemnations of officials who take bribes. Amos says:

> For I know how many are your transgressions
> and how great are your sins—
> you who afflict the righteous, who take a bribe. (Amos 5:12)

The prophet Isaiah of Jerusalem, angry about corruption in the Jerusalem of his day writes:

> Everyone loves a bribe
> and runs after gifts.
> They do not defend the orphan
> and the widow's cause does not come before them. (Isa 1:23)

Isaiah looks back to the time of David's reign as a golden age and hears Yahweh say:

> I will restore your judges as at the first,
>   and your counselors as at the beginning. (Isa 1:26)

As we have said, no legal punishments are specified for taking a bribe. But the practice is identified as odious, and its condemnation appears outside the law collections, in the Psalms (15:5), in Proverbs (6:35), and in the curses that follow the Deuteronomic Code in Deuteronomy (27:25). These citations assist us in uncovering legal administration, even if they do so in a negative way.

Law and the Monarchy

The coming of the monarchy in Israel did not cause an end to the role of village and town elders as judges on the front line of legal proceedings. In the ancient Near East the king was viewed as both a source of divine law and a representative of the gods and their concern for justice. In the Hebrew Bible we have only a few scattered accounts referencing law and the role of the king in its administration. The story of David and the widow of Tekoa is a beautiful account, but extremely literary. The tale of Solomon and the disputed child of two prostitutes is a good example of folklore. And we have mentioned Jehoshaphat above.

The most insightful account of the role of a king in administering law is part of the story of Absalom's rebellion. In 2 Samuel 15 we are informed that Absalom would intercept persons coming from rural areas to Jerusalem to have legal matters judged. He would speak to them in a friendly manner and say:

> "See, your claims are good and right; but there is no one deputed by the king to hear you....If only I were judge in the land! Then all who had a suit or cause might come to me and I would give them justice." (2 Sam 15:3–6)

The implication is that the king, David in this case, had not appointed or deputized a person(s) to deal with these needs. The further implication is that the monarchy was expected to provide a reasonable legal service.

Perhaps the chief impact on the administration of law associated with the monarchy was the establishment of major urban centers of dense population, first at Jerusalem and later in Samaria. Other urban centers grew as time passed. We can assume that a class of professional urban judges grew, with at least some of the chief judges appointed by the king and his advisors as patronage. It is likely that the institution of the monarchy also tried to control the rural areas of the country with the creation of administrative districts.

> Solomon had twelve officials over all Israel, who provided food for the king and his household; each one had to make provision for one month in the year. (1 Kgs 4:7)

Growing urban areas also witnessed the creation of a new merchant class, and laws concerning weights and balances became part of the legal vocabulary. Amos said of the merchants of Samaria:

> We will make the ephah small and the shekel great,
>   and practice deceit with false balances,
> buying the poor for silver
>   and the needy for a pair of sandals,
>   and selling the sweepings of the wheat. (Amos 8:5–6)

The Deuteronomic History is nearly silent on law enforcement, giving us almost no insight into the administration of royal justice, but there is one outstanding account of an event involving Ahab and Jezebel.[5] Jezebel arranged to have Naboth the Jezreelite stoned to obtain his vineyard. She arranged for two false witnesses to testify that Naboth had cursed God and the king (Exod 22:28). Naboth's refusal to surrender his ancestral property to Ahab was in keeping with norms of the time. Naboth was stoned by the elders and nobles of his town in accordance with the form of capital punishment mentioned several times in the laws of the Torah (Lev 24:23, Num 15:36, Deut 21:21).

Were There Prisons?

There are several references to a person being placed in prison. Micaiah, a northern prophet, was placed in prison on bread and water because he would not give the expected advice to the king of Israel (1 Kgs 22:27). Most of the biblical references to prisons are prisons located outside of Israel, in Egypt, for example (Joseph), or Philistia (Samson). Also, the Assyrians are said to have imprisoned Hoshea for seeking an alliance with Egypt. There are also several references to prison in second Isaiah, which would place them in Babylon.

But a review of the many laws of the Torah reveals that there was no mention of a punishment such as imprisonment; no one served time. Penalties included fines of great variety, retribution, including physical harm (a tooth for a tooth), compensation, and death. What this means is that on the occasion of someone breaking the law, a resolution had to be reached, sometimes hurriedly. There may have been no holding areas. Although there may not have been prisons, there are several references to people being held in custody. In Leviticus 24 there is an incident where an Israelite woman's son blasphemed.

> And they put him in custody until the decision of the LORD should be made clear to them. (Lev 24:12)

In Numbers there is a narrative of a man who was placed in custody until it could be determined what his punishment should be for gathering wood on the sabbath day (Num 15:34).

The Role of Priests in the Administration of Justice

We have mentioned the central court located in the place chosen by Yahweh. This was a Deuteronomic concept and in the Deuteronomic Code (Deut 17:8–13) priests who are identified as Levites will be consulted in difficult legal cases, but judges are also mentioned along with the priests:

> ...where you shall consult with the levitical priests and the judge who is in office in those days. (Deut 17:9)

Levitical priests also participate with the elders of the town nearest to where a murdered person is discovered in fulfilling a law concerning an unknown murderer (Deut 21). To fulfill the law all the elders must participate in a recitation[9] beginning with the words:

> "Our hands did not shed this blood, nor were we witnesses to it." (Deut 21:7)

Aaronid priests, who were the official priests of the royal temple, were charged with responsibility concerning the implementation of public health laws related to skin disease and bodily discharges (Lev 13—15). Since the Aaronids were concerned with ritual cleanliness, their charge from the state concerning the enforcement of these laws was logical and provided a valuable service for the general welfare.

Due to the absence of the monarchy in the post-exilic period, there was an increase in the role that the priesthood played in government. Part of this tradition is known to us in the books of Nehemiah and Ezra. Ezra not only represented the Persian monarchy but was known to be a priest. Some scholars think that the passages in the Torah that assign a role to priests in the administration of justice were written back into the scrolls during the post-exilic period.

9

The Laws of the Ancient Near East

Whether there are 613 laws in the Bible or a thousand, they constitute only a small portion of the laws that existed in the political entities of Israel and Judah from the late thirteenth century B.C.E. to the beginning of the sixth century B.C.E., at which time the Chaldeans (neo-Babylonians) put an end to Judah as an independently governed nation. Apart from the Bible we have no examples of Israelite law. All the Israelite laws available to us have been preserved in the scrolls produced by scribes belonging to one or another priesthood.

We are fortunate, however, to have a large number and variety of laws from other cultures of the ancient Near East, laws that were not preserved primarily for theological purposes. While it is outside the purpose of a handbook of biblical law to examine the many law collections at our disposal, we should be familiar with their availability. These collections include the following: the Laws of Ur-Namma (37 laws), the Laws of Lipit-Ishtar (38 laws), the Laws of Eshnunna (60), the Laws of Hammurabi (282), the Neo-Babylonian Laws (15), the Middle Assyrian Laws (105+), the Middle Assyrian Palace Decrees (23 decrees), and the Hittite Laws (200).[1]

Of the above-mentioned law collections, the longest and best organized, the Laws of Hammurabi, was first published in 1902. Hammurabi (sometimes spelled Hammurapi) reigned in Babylon from 1792–50 B.C.E. The best and most famous copy of the Laws of Hammurabi is the black stone stela, a diorite pillar almost eight feet tall, housed at the Louvre in Paris.[2] At the top of the stela is a bas-relief depicting the sun-god Shamash seated on a throne, communicating with Hammurabi. The implication is that together, king and god will promote and protect the divine laws.

LAW COLLECTIONS OF THE ANCIENT NEAR EAST

CHART 9a

Name	Date	Number
Laws of Ur-Namma (LU)	2100 B.C.E.	37
Laws of Lipit-Ishtar (LL)	1930 B.C.E.	38
Laws of Eshnunna (LE)	1770 B.C.E.	60
Laws of Hammurabi (LH)	1750 B.C.E.	282
Hittite Laws (HL)	1650–1500 B.C.E.	200
Middle Assyrian Laws (MAL)	1076 B.C.E.	105+
Middle Assyrian Palace Decrees (MAPD)	1076 B.C.E.	23
Neo-Babylonian Laws (LNB)	700 B.C.E.	15

Prologues and Epilogues

The approximately 280 laws of the Laws of Hammurabi, like the laws of the Covenant Code (Exod 20—23), contain a prologue and an epilogue. This is true also of the Laws of Ur-Namma and the Laws of Lipit-Ishtar. In the prologues, unlike the cultic laws of the Covenant Code, each king is praised as a representative of a god. Ur-namma is called the son of the goddess Ninsun, and Lipit-Ishtar is called the son of the god Enlil. Hammurabi is associated with numerous gods and is praised repeatedly as the pure prince, the lord of kings, shepherd of the people, and the one who gladdens the heart of his divine lord Marduk. The epilogue of the Laws of Hammurabi is an elaborate warning to any who would belittle or destroy the influence or role of Hammurabi in establishing legal justice for the people of Babylon.

The mention of god(s) in the several prologues and epilogues can be misleading, however. In the law collections of the ancient Near East listed above (and in chart 9a) there are almost no laws related to religion, such as the biblical laws concerning festivals, holiness, dietary restrictions, sacrifices, offerings, tithes, vows, priestly behavior, circumcision, or laws requiring the separation of the citizens from *pagans,* or the requirement to destroy the religious apparatus (pillars and posts) of unauthorized religious shrines.[3] This observation concerning the differences between the laws of the Hebrew Bible and the laws of the ancient Near East in general is of vital importance in understanding the biblical laws. We will discuss it further in chapter 10, "Oh, How I Love Your Law!"

Types of Laws in the Law Collections of the Ancient Near East

If the ancient Hittite laws and the laws of Mesopotamia do not deal with religion, what subjects are covered? Here is a partial list in alphabetical order: abortion, adopted children, agricultural disputes, arson, assault, boats, bodily injuries, creditors, debts, false accusations, false witnesses, fines, homicide, inheritance, irrigation, land tenure, livestock, magic, marriage, merchants, prices, property, sexual offenses, slaves, theft, and wages.[4]

Similarities Between the Laws of the Ancient Near East and the Laws of the Bible

It is frequently pointed out that there are easily recognizable similarities between some of the laws of the Bible and the laws of the ancient Near East. This can be expected considering the fact that Israel shared a similar culture with the nations that surrounded her. Were any of the biblical laws copied from other law codes? It cannot be said with certainty that this happened. But we can assume, considering the military activities of Hittites, Egyptians, Assyrians, and Babylonians, and the trade that took place around and in Israel/Judah, that cross-cultural pollination could not have been avoided. There are many striking resemblances and similarities between particular laws of the ancient Near East and those in the Bible. We cite twelve examples:

1. If an engaged woman and a man have illicit sex in the open country (as opposed to the town or city), the woman shall not be punished, because she may have cried out for rescue (Deut 22:23–27). Hittite Law 197 reads:

    > If a citizen rapes a woman while they are in the mountains together, then the sentence for the man is death; the woman is not guilty. If a citizen rapes a woman while they are in her house together, then the sentence for the woman is also death. (HL 197)

2. If an ox gores a person, and the owner was aware that the ox was a gorer, the owner shall be punished (Exod 21:28–29). Similar laws appear in the Laws of Eshnunna and in the Laws of Hammurabi, where fines are specified.

> If an ox is a gorer and the ward authorities so notify its owner, but he fails to keep his ox in check and the ox gores a man and thus causes his death, the owner of the ox shall weigh and deliver forty shekels of silver. (LE 54)

> If the ox of a citizen...even after the city assembly has put the owner on notice that it was dangerous, gores a state official, then the fine is eighteen ounces of silver. (LH 251)

3. In Deuteronomy 19:16–21, if one falsely accuses another of murder without witnesses so the accused can be convicted, the accuser can be put to death. A similar law appears in the Laws of Hammurabi:

> If one citizen charges another with murder, but has no evidence, then the sentence is death. (LH 1)

4. In Exodus 22:2 the punishment for a thief who breaks into a house depends on the time of day. This same distinction is made in the Laws of Eshnunna. In both cases the thief can be put to death if the break-in takes place at night.

> A man who is seized in the house of a commoner, within the house, at midday, shall weigh and deliver ten shekels of silver; he who is seized at night within the house shall die, he will not live. (LE 13)

5. If, during a fight between two men, a woman grabs the testicles of a man, her hand will be amputated (Deut 25:11). In Middle Assyrian Law if a woman crushes a testicle her finger will be cut off. If both testicles are damaged the punishment is more severe.

> If a woman ruptures one of the testicles of a citizen during a fight, then one of her fingers is amputated. If she should crush the second testicle during the quarrel, they shall gouge out both her eyes. (MAL A8)

6. If a man takes a second wife, he shall not diminish the food, clothing, or marital rights of the first wife (Exod 21:10–12). In the Laws of Hammurabi a first wife is entitled to housing and support unless she agrees to move.

> If a man marries a woman, and later...disease seizes her, and he decides to marry another woman, he will not divorce his wife...She shall reside in quarters he constructs, and he shall continue to support her as long as she lives. (LH 148–49)

7. By Torah law a person seeing a lost animal or object lost by a neighbor must protect it until it can be restored (Deut 22:1–3). In Hittite Law there is a similar responsibility:

> If anyone finds an ox, a horse, or a mule, he shall drive it to the king's gate....The finder shall harness it. When its owner finds it, he shall take it according to the law, but he shall not have the finder arrested as a thief. (HL 71)

8. In Numbers 27:8–11 a daughter can inherit from her father. In the Laws of Hammurabi there are seven laws dealing with a daughter's inheritance (178–84). For example,

> If a man does not award a dowry to his daughter who is a *sugitu* and does not give her to a husband, after the father goes to his fate, her brothers shall reward to her a dowry proportionate to the value of the paternal estate, and they shall give her to a husband. (LH 184)

9. In Leviticus 18:23 bestiality is forbidden. In Hittite Law a man who has sex with a cow or a sheep is put to death:

> If a man has sexual relations with a cow, it is an unpermitted sexual pairing; he will be put to death. (HL 187)

> If a man has sexual relations with a sheep, it is an unpermitted sexual pairing; he will be put to death. (HL 188)

10. In Exodus 22:18 a female sorcerer is sentenced to death, and in Leviticus 19:26 witchcraft is forbidden. In Middle Assyrian Law a man or a woman practicing witchcraft is sentenced to death:

> If either a man or a woman shall be discovered practicing witchcraft, and if they prove the charges against them...they shall kill the practitioner of witchcraft. (MAL A47)

11. In Exodus 22:5 a person who allows his livestock to graze in another's field shall make restitution. In the Laws of Hammurabi a similar law deals with a person who allows his sheep or goats to graze in someone's field without permission:

> If a shepherd does not make an agreement with the owner of the field to graze sheep and goats, and without permission of the owner of the field grazes sheep and goats on the field, the owner of the field shall harvest his field and the shepherd who grazed sheep and goats on the field without permission of the owner of the field shall give in addition 6,000 silas of grain per ikus (of field) to the owner of the field. (LH 57)

Also, in Exodus 22:6 a law dealing with a fire that damages a neighbor's field follows the grazing law. Curiously, an anti-grazing law and a fire-damage law appear together in the Hittite Laws (106–7).

12. In Deuteronomy 19:14 and 27:17 boundary markers for property are made sacred. In Middle Assyrian Law a boundary violation invokes a severe fine:

> If a man should incorporate a large border area of his comrade's property into his own and they prove the charges against him and find him guilty, he shall give a field triple that which he had incorporated; they shall strike him 100 blows with rods; he shall perform the king's service for one full month. (MAL B8)

The above-mentioned similarities, and others, are worth knowing. But it is often pointed out that the differences between the biblical laws and the other law collections of the ancient Near East are more pronounced than the parallels. And the chief difference, which we cannot overlook, is the way the Torah laws are blended into the narrative of Yahweh's salvation history. The laws of the Torah are presented to us as the laws of Yahweh, not the laws of custom or the mere laws of Moses. God communicates laws to the people in a way that has no parallel in other law collections of the ancient Near East.[5]

10

Oh, How I Love Your Law!

There was no culture of ancient times where the law was studied, memorized, sought after, and actually loved as it was in the restored, post-captivity Jewish community of Judah.

> If your law had not been my delight,
>   I would have perished in my misery.
> I will never forget your precepts,
>   for by them you have given me life.
> Oh, how I love your law!
>   It is my meditation all day long. (Ps 119:92–93, 97)

In Psalm 119 the author praised the laws of Yahweh 176 times. There is nothing like that in ancient or modern literature. We must ask ourselves how this came to pass. We begin with the final destruction of Jerusalem by the Chaldeans in 587–86 B.C.E.

The first two decades of the sixth century B.C.E. were years of devastation. The temple was plundered and destroyed, the walls of the city breached, and the king was captured and tortured.

> They slaughtered the sons of Zedekiah before his eyes, then put out the eyes of Zedekiah; they bound him in fetters and took him to Babylon. (2 Kgs 25:7)

When the Judahite captives arrived in Babylon, they could not possibly have foreseen any hope in their future. But time passed and amazingly some wounds began to heal. In a letter attributed to Jeremiah, this advice was given:

> Build houses and live in them; plant gardens and eat what they produce. Take wives and have sons and daughters. (Jer 29:5–6)

Eventually the Aaronid priests of the former temple of Yahweh regained their balance. In their past was a brutalized people, a destroyed city, and a defiled temple. The people looked to the priests for answers, and fortunately the priests had been able to save a variety of writings. These writings first became interesting but soon became precious. They were studied, searched, memorized, and adored. Slowly the Jews became "people of the book."

The Pentateuch

The Aaronid priests had first witnessed the power of the written word when the book of the law had been discovered during the reign of Josiah. Shortly thereafter an idealized history of Israel appeared, the work of a marginal priesthood that traced its origins to the destroyed northern kingdom. This history had started with Joshua and had ended with Josiah.

The Aaronid priests were greatly impressed by the writings of the Shechemite Levites.[1] Seeing a viable opportunity to preserve the identity of the people of Yahweh, they decided to produce new scrolls to meet new needs. They already had in their possession many resources, including the work of three literary groups whom scholars have called the Yahwist, the Elohist, and the Deuteronomist. They also had some collections of laws along with a manual of priestly procedures and concerns. They decided to blend the narratives of important traditions with collections of secular law and sacred commandments.[2] Influenced by Babylonian culture, they decided to begin their scrolls with a creation account. They produced the magnificent theological tone poem found in Genesis chapter 1. Immediately thereafter, in what is now called chapters 2 and 3, we discover one of their practices. Following their own account of creation, they included another creation story, one that differed from their own in feeling, vocabulary, and theology, the account of Adam and Eve attributed to the Yahwist. The practice of the priestly authors was to include important material deemed too valuable to omit, even if it did not harmonize with their own. They continued this throughout the Tetrateuch. In this example they put the two differing creation accounts back to back. In other places, such as the story of the flood, they dovetailed their own account with another, also attributed to the Yahwist. There are many examples of conflicting facts in their masterwork,[3] but consistency took a back seat to inclusion.

Was the priestly party perfect? Were its members all of one mind? Probably not. In a recent study of the exilic and post-exilic period Rainer Albertz writes:

> We should certainly not imagine the priesthood of the early post-exilic period as a homogenous group.[4]

With this in mind perhaps we can account for the composition of the Holiness Code, which seems to differ in some ways from the Priestly Code to which it is related (see chapters 4 and 5).

At any rate, the scrolls that the priests created included a blending of narrative and law. Perhaps the scattering of the Priestly Code itself was an attempt to keep the narrative moving and not lose it completely. In addition to the Priestly Code and the Holiness Code we find the Covenant Code and the several decalogues that complement each other in Exodus 20 and Exodus 34.

While many facts concerning the completion of the Tetrateuch are unclear, understanding can be enhanced by raising questions. When the Aaronid priests first put together the Tetrateuch, did they have any idea how precious it would eventually become to the dispersed people of God? In the stages of putting together their literary creation, did they basically include everything they had or did they carefully select material that met their criteria and discard other material? If they had Deuteronomy before they started, as many scholars believe, did they plan early on to include it at the completion of their efforts, and if so how did it influence their literary decisions? Or was it much later in the post-exilic period that the decision was made to remove the book of Deuteronomy from its place at the beginning of the Deuteronomic scrolls collection and place it at the end of the Tetrateuch to complete a Pentateuch? Even though the Deuteronomic Code differed in obvious ways from the law codes of the first four books,[5] it was simply too valuable to ignore. To some of our questions there are no answers. As Roland Murphy says, "The formation of these books is still shrouded in mystery."[6]

But their product is one of the wonders of the ancient world. Their combined work of law and narrative changed the defeated nation of Jews into a remnant of hope and faith. The law, of all things, became a source of joy.

> The law of the LORD is perfect,
>   reviving the soul;
> the decrees of the LORD are sure,
>   making wise the simple;
> the precepts of the LORD are right,
>   rejoicing the heart;
> the commandment of the LORD is clear,
>   enlightening the eyes....
> More to be desired are they than gold,
>   even much fine gold;
> sweeter also than honey,
>   and drippings of the honeycomb. (Ps 19:7–8, 10)

Our knowledge of the law collections of other nations of the ancient Near East has expanded in recent years, but nowhere do we find intense statements of love and joy associated with the possession of law as we do in the Hebrew Bible. And in no other culture do we find the law as an intimate revelation of a concerned and loving God. The law for the Jew, since the post-exilic period, has been a source of great joy, as anyone knows who has attended the synagogue ceremony called *simhat tora* (joy of the Torah). We must read with understanding the opening words of Israel's ancient hymnbook, the book of Psalms, when it describes those who are happy and righteous:

> Their delight is in the law of the LORD,
>   and on his law they meditate day and night. (Ps 1:2)

Appendix:
Laws in the Book of Genesis

There are no law codes as such in Genesis, but laws from the various codes and collections of historical Israel are reflected and referred to in the Genesis narratives.[1] We will briefly discuss these legal references as they appear in the three sections of Genesis: (1) stories of the ancient world (1—11); (2) the patriarchs of Israel (12—36); and (3) the sons of Jacob (37—50).

Stories of the Ancient World

Be Fertile and Multiply

Most scholars date the authorship of the magnificent priestly account of creation (Gen 1—2:4a) to the sixth century B.C.E. during the decades of the Babylonian captivity. Two basic priestly laws appear as the powerful poetic account unfolds. At the end of the sixth day of creation the first commandment from God to humans is given:

> God blessed them, and God said to them: "Be fertile and multiply, and fill the earth and subdue it." (Gen 1:28)

This is a basic priestly concern, and in the opening of the second book of the Torah, Exodus, we read these words from the priestly source:

> The Israelites were fruitful and prolific; they multiplied and grew exceedingly strong. (Exod 2:7)

First Mention of the Sabbath

After six days of creation activity, a day of rest is instituted:

> God blessed the seventh day and hallowed it, because on it God rested
> from all the work he had done in creation. (Gen 2:3)

When the command to keep the sabbath appears in the Ethical Decalogue
of Exodus 20, it is tied to the creation account of Genesis by this editorial
comment:

> For in six days the LORD made heaven and earth, the sea, and all that is
> in them, but rested the seventh day. (Exod 20:11)

However, when the same commandment appears in Deuteronomy (chapter
5), no mention whatsoever is made of the creation of the world in six days.
The exhortatory remark in Deuteronomy that explains the command concerning the keeping of the sabbath is as follows:

> Remember that you were a slave in the land of Egypt, and the LORD
> your God brought you out from there with a mighty hand and an out-
> stretched arm; therefore the LORD your God commanded you to keep
> the sabbath day. (Deut 5:15)

The First Murder

After the expulsion of Adam and Eve from the garden, we are told of
the birth of the first two children: Cain, a farmer, and Abel, a shepherd.
When they are grown, angry feelings on the part of Cain toward God and
Abel lead to the first murder. The reader rightly perceives that Cain knew
that he had committed an unlawful, act even though there is no mention in
early Genesis of a particular law prohibiting murder.

Animals, Clean and Unclean

When the impatience of God with humanity leads to the flood, it is not
because humans refuse to obey his laws. The narrator simply states:

> The LORD saw that the wickedness of humankind was great in the earth,
> and that every inclination of the thoughts of their hearts was only evil
> continually. (Gen 6:5)

An interesting aspect of the Noah story is related to the instructions given to
Noah by God:

> Take with you *seven* pairs of all clean animals, the male and its mate; and a [single] pair of the animals that are not clean. (Gen 7:2; emphasis added)

It seems as if the redactor has forgotten that the distinction between clean animals and unclean animals is not made to Israel until the law is given in the wilderness following the nation's deliverance from Egypt (see Lev 11:24–47; Lev 20; Deut 14:3–21).

The Patriarchs of Israel

First Mention of the Tithe

References to laws given to Israel at Sinai and in the wilderness appear sporadically in the patriarchal narratives. For example, in Genesis 14 we are told that Abram gave Melchizedek, a priest of God Most High, a tenth of everything that he had (14:18–20). This is the only mention of the tithe before the book of Leviticus (Lev 27; see also Num 18 and Deut 12).

Circumcision

The most extensive reference to a requirement of the law appears in the priestly chapter 17 of Genesis, where the act of circumcision is commanded by God.

> Throughout your generations every male among you shall be circumcised when he is eight days old....Any uncircumcised male who is not circumcised in the flesh of his foreskin shall be cut off from his people; he has broken my covenant. (Gen 17:12–14)

The emphasis on circumcision in this priestly chapter is in keeping with the exilic Aaronid strategy of establishing and preserving a Judean identity for the exiles. Circumcision had been widely practiced in Egypt and the regions bordering the eastern Mediterranean (Israel, Edom, Moab) but was not practiced in Mesopotamia by Assyrians, Babylonians, or Chaldeans. In Genesis 17 circumcision is incorporated into the Abraham saga as the sign of a covenant between God and Abraham's descendants. The word *covenant* is used no fewer than thirteen times in this chapter.[2]

Intermarriage with Canaanites

Laws enter the narratives of the patriarchal period in many ways. A law in Deuteronomy forbids Israelites to marry the original inhabitants of the land. It is reflected in a Jacob tradition in which Rebekah, Esau's and Jacob's mother, expresses her anger about Esau's marrying of Canaanite women (Gen

27:46; see 26:34–35). In this tradition Jacob goes to Paddan-aram to marry one of his own kin, not to flee the wrath of a cheated Esau. Isaac, under the influence of Rebekah, says to Jacob:

> "You shall not marry one of the Canaanite women. Go at once to Paddan-aram…and take as a wife from there one of the daughters of Laban, your mother's brother." (Gen 28:1–2)

Marriage with Sisters Forbidden

The Jacob tradition has Jacob marrying sisters, Leah and Rachel. Leviticus 18:18 reads:

> You shall not take a woman as a rival to her sister…while her sister is still alive.

Scholars are quick to remind us that Jacob lived centuries before this law from Leviticus was given.

The Building of Altars

Laws in the Torah concerning the building of altars are conflicting. In Exodus 20 Israelites are encouraged to build altars for animal sacrifices "in every place where I cause my name to be remembered." In Genesis, altars are built at various locations by Noah, Abraham, Isaac, and Jacob.

In Deuteronomy 12 one central, solitary altar is required by law for all Israel.

THE BUILDING OF ALTARS IN GENESIS

CHART A1

Scripture	Builder	Location
8:20	Noah	Ararat
12:8	Abraham	Near Bethel
13:18	Abraham	Hebron
22:9	Abraham	Mount Moriah
26:25	Isaac	Beersheba
33:20	Jacob	Shechem
35:1	Jacob	Bethel

> Take care that you do not offer your burnt offerings at any place you happen to see. But only at the place that the LORD will choose in one of your tribes… (Deut 12:13–14)

In the Holiness Code the opening law is basic (Lev 17:1–5). Sacrifices can only be made at the tent of meeting where the Aaronid priests officiate. The tent is identified as the dwelling of the Lord. The ancient historical practice of individual sacrifice is referred to, however:

> This is in order that the people of Israel may bring their sacrifices that they offer in the open field, that they may bring them to the LORD, to the priest at the entrance of the tent of meeting, and offer them as sacrifices of well-being to the LORD. (Lev 17:5)[3]

The Rape of an Unengaged Woman

In Genesis 34 the daughter of Leah and Jacob, Dinah, is raped by Shechem, son of Hamor the Hivite. Torah law states that a man who rapes an unengaged woman must marry her and pay her father the marriage price (Exod 22:15; Deut 22:28). Shechem indeed wants to marry Dinah, but we read that her brothers were outraged.

> When they [the brothers] heard of it, the men were indignant and very angry, because he had committed an outrage in Israel by lying with Jacob's daughter; such a thing ought not to be done. (Gen 34:7)

A lengthy story of revenge follows in which the city of Shechem is sacked and many are killed and kidnapped by sons of Jacob.

First Mention of a Food Taboo

In Genesis 32 we encounter a story of Jacob returning home to Caanan after his lengthy stay with Laban. This story combines three folk etiologies,[4] one of which involves a food taboo that is counted as a law by rabbinical tradition.[5] Jacob is said to have wrestled all night with a man (or God) and leaves the encounter with a blessing, a new name, Israel, and a pronounced limp because of an injury to his hip.

> Therefore to this day the Israelites do not eat the thigh muscle that is on the hip socket, because he struck Jacob on the hip socket at the thigh muscle. (Gen 32:32)

A Law Concerning Relations with Edomites

A law in Deuteronomy reads:

> You shall not abhor any of the Edomites, for they are your kin. (Deut 23:7)

Genesis 36 explains in great detail how the Edomites are the descendants of Esau, Jacob's brother.

The Sons of Jacob

Levirate Marriage

Stories of Jacob's family (especially Joseph) are found in Genesis 37—50. In chapter 38 we have an incident referring to the practice of the levirate marriage law of Deuteronomy 25:5–10.[6] This law states that if an Israelite man dies childless, his brother is obligated to marry the widow to continue his brother's line. The law also includes a description of a procedure to be followed by the widow if the living brother refuses to marry her (see Ruth 4). The Genesis story is a strange variation of the levirate law. The brother who died without children, Er, the son of Judah, is said to have been put to death by the LORD. Judah spoke to his second son, Onan:

> "Go in to your brother's wife and perform the duty of a brother-in-law to her; raise up offspring for your brother." (Gen 38:8)

Onan avoids his responsibility. "He spilled his semen on the ground," and it is said that the Lord "put him to death also" (Gen 38:9–10).

A Prohibited Sexual Encounter

Following the above incident is a story of how Tamar tricked Judah into breaking the law prohibiting a sexual encounter with a daughter-in-law (Lev 18:15; 20:21).

Adultery

An important event of the Joseph novella has Joseph refusing to commit adultery with Potiphar's wife and subsequently being confined to the king's prison (Gen 39).

Summary

While it is widely believed that the book of Genesis reached its canonical form during or following the Babylonian exile, the book contains very ancient oral traditions from various locations in Judah and Israel. No law code is identified in Genesis, but, as we have illustrated above, laws of later periods frequently surfaced in the preservation of ancient traditions. In the opening chapters of Genesis, God is reported to have given specific commands to Adam and Eve, and later God confronts Cain following the murder of his brother. When the flood comes from God as punishment, it is not stated that humans were punished because they did not keep the laws of God.

The priestly editors used many sources when they compiled Genesis as the first book of their magnificent scroll collection, but it is obvious that Genesis 17 is solely a priestly creation inserted in the Abraham saga. Here God speaks directly to Abraham. Circumcision is established as a requirement for all Israelite males as a sign of a special covenant between God Almighty and the descendants of Abraham. The word *covenant* when used by the P source does not imply the vassal treaty structure of Deuteronomy. Circumcision was an important key element in the priestly program to contribute to the establishment of the identity of displaced Judeans of the exilic period.

Notes

1. The Religion of Judah Becomes Preoccupied with Law

1. The references to the reading of the law by Josiah and Ezra are historical. The references to Moses and Joshua are theological projections into Israel's re-created past. There is an interesting reference to the teachings of the book of the law during the reign of Jehoshaphat (873–849) found in 2 Chronicles 17. The origin of this tradition needs further research.

2. The northern kingdom, Israel, was destroyed in 722 B.C.E. by the Assyrians. Many northerners fled to Judah in the south. Judah outlasted Israel by more than a century.

3. For the comparison scholars have made between Joshua and Josiah, see William J. Doorly, *Obsession with Justice, The Story of the Deuteronomists* (Mahwah, N.J.: Paulist Press, 1994), 37–45.

4. We do not believe that the subservient relationship of Levites to Aaronids (where Aaronids are called priests), as set forth in the books of Exodus, Leviticus, Numbers, and Chronicles, existed during the reign of Josiah (640–609 B.C.E.).

5. J stands for Yahwist (from Jahwist, the German spelling of this name), E for Elohist, and D for Deuteronomist.

6. There is no historical base for this setting. The first Israelites were Canaanites involved in a population shift; they resettled in the highlands late in the thirteenth century from the surrounding areas.

7. The root of the Hebrew name Horeb portrays a dry, desolate area like a desert. In the Deuteronomic tradition it is probable that Horeb was not a mountain at all but an area. During the exile, when the royal

priests put together the scroll of Exodus, Horeb was declared to be the mountain of God. So in Exodus 3:1 we read, "Horeb, the mountain of God" (Thomas Dozeman, *God on the Mountain,* [Atlanta, Ga.: Scholars Press, 1989], 68–72).

8. The word *Sinai* only appears once in the book of Deuteronomy. It is in chapter 33, a late addition to the scroll. The name Sinai does not appear in Joshua at all. In Deuteronomy the name Horeb for the mountain, or the area where the tradition says the law was given, appears nine times.

2. The Covenant Code

1. The start of this collection in the canonical scriptures is Exodus 20:22, "The LORD said to Moses." An earlier version started with Exodus 21:1, "These are the ordinances that you shall set before them." The original final law was "You shall not boil a kid in its mother's milk" (Exod 23:19). The blessings under the heading ("I am going to send an angel in front of you…to bring you to the place that I have prepared," Exod 23:20) were not part of the original collection of laws.

2. Scholars come up with different totals. We reach the number fifty-two as follows. The cultic preamble contains four laws. Part I contains twenty-two, Part II contains twenty, and the cultic conclusion, eight. The number fifty-two is reached if the three annual festivals are listed under one law, "Three times in the year you shall hold a festival for me" (Exod 23:14–17). We explain our numbers with the charts and text in this chapter. The rabbinical tradition concerning 613 laws in the Torah assigns fifty-four laws to the Covenant Code (see chapter 6, "The Rabbinical Tradition of 613 Laws").

3. The famous law code of Hammurabi (1792–1750 B.C.E.) contains more than two hundred laws along with a prologue and an epilogue. It is the largest law collection of ancient times (Mesopotamia), and we know that some sections are missing (see chapter 9, "The Laws of the Ancient Near East").

4. Gosta W. Ahlstrom casts doubt on the historicity of Hezekiah's reform (*The History of Ancient Palestine* [Minneapolis, Minn.: Fortress Press, 1993], 701–5). Rainer Albertz supports the historicity of the Hezekian reform and suggests that the Book of the Covenant was used to promote the reform of Hezekiah (*A History of Israelite Religion* [Louisville, Ky.: Westminster/John Knox Press, 1994], 180–86).

5. The Hebrew word for covenant, *BRT*, has been reproduced in English with a variety of spellings, *berith, beyrith, brith,* and *berit.* Regardless of the English spelling the same Hebrew word is represented.

6. The collection of law we are discussing became known as the Book of the Covenant because of the section concerning Moses that appears in Exodus 24:7, where it is stated that Moses read from the "book of the covenant."

7. See Brevard Childs, *Exodus* (Philadelphia: Westminster Press, 1974), 453.

8. Donald B. Redford, *Egypt, Canaan, and Israel in Ancient Times* (Princeton, N.J.: Princeton University Press, 1992), 408–22. Redford identifies the politics and geography of the Egypt represented in the book of Exodus as belonging to the 26th dynasty, when Psammetichus became pharaoh. This would date the canonical book of Exodus in the neo-Babylonian and early Persian period at the end of the exile.

9. In the authentic oracles of Isaiah of Jerusalem, Amos, and Micah there is no emphasis on the exodus tradition. There is actually a preexilic passage in Amos that belittles the Israelite exodus tradition (Amos 9:7–8).

10. It is widely believed that the J source and the E source may have been already merged before being used by the exilic priests in their production of the scroll of Exodus. The merged sources are referred to as JE.

11. The editorial complexities of the book of Exodus are vast and it is not in our interest to further explore them in this text. The reader is referred to the *New Jerome Biblical Commentary* (Englewood Cliffs, N.J.: Prentice Hall, 1990), 44–60; Childs, *Exodus;* and Dozeman, *God on the Mountain.*

12. We are about to begin a discussion of the two parts of the Book of the Covenant that we will call Part I and Part II. These two parts originated separately.

13. Ronald E. Clements, *The Cambridge Bible Commentary, Exodus* (Cambridge, England: Cambridge University Press, 1972), 128.

14. Gerhard Von Rad, *Deuteronomy,* 4th ed. (Philadelphia: Westminster Press, 1975), 14; Doorly, *Obsession with Justice,* 154–55.

15. Clements, *Exodus,* 128. Clements suggests that the Book of the Covenant is connected with the Shechem shrine. Also see Norman

Gottwald in his article on Old Testament law codes in *The Interpreter's One Volume Commentary on the Bible* (Nashville, Tenn.: Abingdon Press, 1971), 1093.

16. There are scholars who believe that the section explaining the three annual festivals in the conclusion of the Book of the Covenant, in which all male members of the community must participate (Exod 23:14–17), is the back end of a bracket of which the laws of the altar constitute the front end.

17. It seems that the wearing of undergarments was not widespread in ancient Israel.

18. The laws found in Part I, Exodus 21:2—22:17, are often called the *mishpatim.* The Hebrew word *mishpatim* is often translated "ordinances."

19. An interesting explanation of the casuistic laws is that these laws were not directed to the citizens (as were apodictic laws) but to judges who would be guided by them in making judicial decisions.

20. There are always exceptions when examining biblical law in its canonical form. There are three laws in the middle of the first half of the Book of the Covenant (Part I) that cannot be called casuistic and do not employ the when and if clauses. These laws are found in Exodus 21:15–17.

21. There is one exception to this statement. In Exodus 21:12, in a law dealing with unpremeditated murder, we read, "I will appoint for you a place to which the killer may flee." In the next verse (part of the same paragraph) we have reference to "my altar." Brevard Childs says that verse 12 is the first verse of a serious interpolation (*Exodus*, 454).

22. We have fragments of non-Israelite law codes from the ancient Near East. These include laws of Ur-namma, Lipit-Ishtar, Eshnunna, Hammurabi; Middle Assyrian laws; Middle-Assyrian palace decrees; and others. We will discuss these collections in chapter 9, "The Laws of the Ancient Near East."

23. Albecht Alt's definition of apodictic law has had a great influence on the study of Old Testament law. His description of apodictic law as being somewhat uniquely Israelite has been challenged, however.

24. Brevard Childs suggests that words reminding readers of an exodus experience in their past (Exod 22:21, 23:9, 23:15) are probably Deuteronomic glosses (*Exodus*, 454–55).

25. David Hopkins, *The Highlands of Canaan: Agriculture in the Early Iron Age* (Sheffield, UK: JSOT Press, 1985), 192–97. Hopkins states

that the land would have to lie fallow every second year to restore productivity.

26. In the Exodus version of the sabbath commandment (Exod 20:8–11) observance is tied to the creation myth of the Priestly chapter 1 of Genesis. *Elohim* rested on the seventh day, therefore the seventh day is a day of rest.

27. There is an Ugaritic fragment containing the words "cook a kid in milk" (see Childs, *Exodus,* 485–86).

28. It is interesting to note that the same three laws that end the Covenant Code (Exod 23:18–19) also end the so-called Ritual Decalogue of Exodus 34. So the final law of each is the prohibition concerning the kid in its mother's milk.

3. The Law Code of Deuteronomy

1. For a discussion of the stages of the growth of the scroll of Deuteronomy, see Doorly, *Obsession with Justice,* 99–117.

2. Chapter 13 contains three situations where attempts are made to lead Israel away from Yahweh. Whether this activity is carried out by false prophets, a friend or close family member, or a whole town, the instigators are to be put to death.

3. The group responsible for carrying out the destruction of the guilty town is not described or identified. Also, the law speaks of a group that would *inquire and make a thorough investigation.* There is no record of any such investigative body existing in Israel.

4. Rabbi Joseph Telushkin, *Biblical Literacy* (New York: William Morrow, 1997), 567–91.

5. Gottwald, *The Interpreter's One Volume Commentary on the Bible,* 1092.

6. We will be discussing the Holiness Code in chapter 4. There are those who believe that the Holiness Code could have appeared earlier in Judah than the reign of Josiah, in which case it would not be correct to say that the Deuteronomic Code was the first law code. It is our view that if the Holiness Code did appear before the reign of Josiah, it did not have the impact it would later have during and after the captivity period.

7. Von Rad, *Deuteronomy,* 19–20.

8. A command to love the alien is also found in the Holiness Code (see Lev 19:34).

9. There are biblical hints that in the history of the northern territory there were Levitical efforts to centralize the worship of Yahweh for an area of Israel first at Shechem (Josh 8:30) and later at Shiloh (Jer 7:12).

10. It is essential—and interesting—to note that the author of this initial law refers to the altars, pillars, sacred poles, and idols by using the word "their." It was *their* altars, *their* pillars, *their* sacred poles, and so forth. The Deuteronomic lawgiver, along with the Deuteronomic historian, creates the fiction that Israel was separate from all these practices from the very beginning (six hundred years before Josiah) and that Israel became corrupted by Canaanite practices of the people living in Canaan. While there is a great theological strategy at work here, it would not be historically possible to substantiate the Deuteronomic assertions.

11. Von Rad, *Deuteronomy*, 89.

12. In the Deuteronomic Code proper Sinai is not mentioned, and the name Horeb appears only once (Deut 18:16).

13. There is no law requiring the observance of the sabbath day in chapters 12—26. The sabbath is mentioned three times in Deuteronomy 5, but this chapter is an exilic addition to the scroll of Deuteronomy.

4. The Holiness Code

1. A fact often overlooked in mentioning the demand for the holiness of Israel in the Holiness Code is that the demand for holiness appears in the Priestly Code *before* the collection of laws found in Leviticus 17–26. For example, see Leviticus 11:44–45: "I am the LORD your God; sanctify yourselves therefore, and be holy, for I am holy....You shall be holy, for I am holy."

2. Susan Ackerman, *Under Every Green Tree* (Atlanta, Ga.: Scholars Press, 1992), 211–12. In several paragraphs she is able to highlight the several aspects of the term *holy*.

3. Frank Crusemann, *The Torah: Theology and Social History of the Old Testament* (Minneapolis, Minn.: Fortress Press, 1996), 300.

4. Ackerman, *Under Every Green Tree*, 210–12.

5. We notice that in the Priestly Code and the Holiness Code the tent or tabernacle is the place of Yahweh's presence. In Deuteronomy we note that the sanctuary is not the place of Yahweh's dwelling, but only the place where his *name* dwells.

6. It is true that there are sections of the Holiness Code that seem inappropriate for public reading inasmuch as they are primarily concerned with priestly matters. An example would be the section on sacred donations (Lev 22). We have to keep in mind that the Holiness Code as we have it is the canonical version with additions to an earlier, shorter version. So, why were some of these strictly priestly sections added to the Holiness Code?

7. The author of the Holiness Code is projecting the origin of this body of law into Israel's distant past during the wilderness period. These words are the words of Yahweh to Moses. Israel is assumed to be encamped somewhere in the Sinai peninsula. When we get to Leviticus 17:8, however, there is mention of the aliens who live among the Israelites. It is our opinion that verse 8 is a gloss.

8. There are numerous scholarly positions concerning the time of the appearance of the Holiness Code. Roland J. Faley proposes that the Holiness Code appeared after Josiah, during the last days of Jerusalem before the exile (*New Jerome Biblical Commentary,* 72). Frank Crusemann proposes the exile as the time of its appearance (*The Torah,* 282–94). Jacob Milgrom states that it made its first appearance prior to the reign of Josiah, with finishing touches provided during the exile (*Leviticus 1—16,* vol. 3 of the Anchor Bible [New York: Doubleday, 1991], 13–29).

9. I. Knohl, *The Concept of God and Cult in the Priestly Torah and in the Holiness School,* Ph.D. diss., Hebrew University, 1988.

10. Jan Joosten, *People and Land in the Holiness Code* (Leiden: E. J. Brill, 1996).

11. Milgrom, *Leviticus 1–16,* 9–10.

12. Milgrom, *Leviticus 1–16,* 27.

13. We can speculate on the reasons why the two lists were not combined. Perhaps one list had to do with holiness and the other list, containing sanctions, had to do with civil law. It is possible that these two lists were entered into the scroll for the future use of the Aaronid priesthood only, and that the scribes did not foresee the production of multiple copies of the scroll that would eventually lead to study and analysis by students and questioning scholars of future generations.

14. Tikva Frymer-Kensky, "Law and Philosophy: The Case of Sex in the Bible," *Semeia* 45 (Atlanta, Ga.: Scholars Press, 1989), 98–99.

15. Simply put, a cultic law deals with a human's relationship with God, and a social or secular law deals with a relationship or interaction with

other humans on a day-to-day basis. In each law collection the subject matter keeps switching from cultic requirements to secular ordinances, and the Holiness Code is no exception. For example, Leviticus 19 contains approximately seventeen cultic laws and thirty secular laws. An example of a cultic law is "Do not turn to idols or make cast images for yourselves" (v. 4). Examples of secular laws are "You shall not defraud your neighbor; you shall not steal; you shall not keep for yourselves the wages of a laborer until morning" (v. 13). By our count the Holiness Code contains sixty-eight cultic laws, eighty secular laws, and thirteen laws that may be counted either way.

16. Milgrom, *Leviticus 1–16*, 27.

17. Hans Boecker, *Law and the Administration of Justice in the Old Testament* (Minneapolis, Minn.: Augsburg, 1980), 188–89.

18. Lawrence Boadt, "Ezekiel," *New Jerome Biblical Commentary*, 307.

5. The Priestly Code

1. Some scholars consider the Holiness Code part of the Priestly Code.

2. Although the *Tanakh* and the *NRSV* read *"burnt offerings,"* the *New American Bible* consistently translates the Hebrew *(olah)* as "holocausts."

3. In chapter 10 there is a priestly law forbidding the consumption of strong drink before entering the sanctuary (Lev 10:9). Perhaps the implication is that when Aaron's two sons offered profane fire they were intoxicated.

4. Contrast the elaborate details of Leviticus 13—15 with the simplicity of the leprous skin disease law of the Deuteronomic Code: "Guard against an outbreak of a leprous skin disease by being very careful; you shall carefully observe whatever the Levitical priests instruct you" (Deut 24:8).

5. See the story of Naaman and Elisha (2 Kgs 5) and the story of four leprous men (2 Kgs 7).

6. In chapter 6, "The Rabbinical Tradition of 613 Laws," we will discuss law 185, which is based on Leviticus 16 and is the basis for priestly rituals for Yom Kippur. Law 313 establishes Yom Kippur as a national day of observance and is based on Leviticus 23:27.

7. Telushkin, *Biblical Literacy*, 561.

8. What is interesting about this law is that it is not typical of priestly laws, most of which relate to priestly responsibilities and concerns.

9. Milgrom, *The Interpreter's One Volume Commentary on the Bible*, 81.

10. The Levites did not share these views of Yahweh's concerns. For one thing, Yahweh did not dwell in Jerusalem. Jerusalem was the place chosen by Yahweh for his *name* to dwell.

11. In the early years of the captivity Jeremiah had written a letter to the captives telling them to settle down and make Babylon their home, raise their families, and seek the welfare of the city where they found themselves (Jer 29:1–14). Jeremiah assumed that the Judahites would be anxious to return to Jerusalem after seventy years, but that was not the case for many families of the deportees.

12. Robert and Mary Coote, *Power, Politics, and the Making of the Bible* (Minneapolis, Minn.: Augsburg/Fortress Press, 1990), 71.

13. The expression "be fruitful and multiply" is one that identifies the priestly source. These are the first words of God to man and woman after their creation in Genesis 1:28.

14. An interesting reference concerning sabbath observance can be found in the book of Amos. Amos, speaking of exploitation by merchants, ties the sabbath with the month rather than the week.

> Hear this, you that trample on the needy...
> saying, "When will the new moon be over
> so that we may sell grain;
> and the sabbath,
>   so that we may offer wheat for sale? (Amos 8:5)

15. There was no reference to creation in six days in the earlier Deuteronomic version of the fourth commandment (Deut 5:12–15).

16. In Deuteronomy circumcision is not required. There circumcision is spiritualized: "Circumcise, then, the foreskin of your heart,...the LORD your God will circumcise your heart" (Deut 10:16; 30:6).

17. Read Exodus 28 and 39.

18. A. D. H. Mayes, *The New Century Bible Commentary, Deuteronomy* (Grand Rapids, Mich.: Eerdmans, 1981), 239–43. The principle behind the dietary laws is explained thoroughly from the Aaronid viewpoint several places in the Tetrateuch, including Leviticus 11:24–47. This explanation is not found in the oldest collection of laws, the Covenant Code (Exod 20:22—23:19). The principle does appear in Deuteronomy 14:3–21. Mayes states that the Deuteronomic passage has been extended by an editor influenced by the Leviticus passage.

19. What role the exodus played in Jerusalem theology before the exile is not certain. For example, looking back we see that the exodus was not important to Isaiah of Jerusalem.

20. Of course we are familiar with the substitution of a ram at God's command for Isaac, the son of Abraham (Gen 22:13).

21. Martin Noth, *A History of Pentateuchal Traditions* (Atlanta, Ga.: The Scholars Press, 1981). Noth and other scholars have demonstrated in many writings that traditions which now compose the Pentateuch were separate traditions that were knit together. These include exodus, wilderness, and Sinai traditions. Any one of these could have been part of the traditions of a group or several groups that joined the historical Israel early, in the days before the monarchy. These traditions grew during the monarchy and appeared in the J source, the E source, and may also have existed in other sources, both oral and written, throughout the rural areas of Israel and Judah. In their present form they are entirely theologized.

22. Peter F. Ellis, *The Men and the Message of the Old Testament* (Collegeville, Minn.: The Liturgical Press, 1963), 69–70. Scholars assign much of the narrative of Numbers to the JE source. Ellis assigns entire chapters to JE, including Numbers 11, 14, 21, 22, 23, and 24.

6. The Rabbinical Tradition of 613 Laws

1. The first two sections of the Jewish Bible are the Torah and the Nevi'im, that is, the five books of Moses and the Prophets (including the Deuteronomic History).

2. Babylonian Talmud, Makkot 23b.

3. Maimonides's work is called *Sefer ha-Mitzvot* (The Book of the Commandments) and haLevi's work is entitled *Sefer ha-Hinnuch* (The Book of Education).

4. Abraham Chill, *The Mitzvot, The Commandments and Their Rationale* (New York: Bloch Publishing Company, 1974), xiv–xviii.

5. Telushkin, *Biblical Literacy*, 526.

6. There is no verse in Leviticus that specifically prohibits sex with a daughter, but it appears in the *Sefer ha-Hinnuch* (law 195) and is demanded by moral logic.

7. Jewish commentary identifies this as a prohibition of a homosexual relationship between an uncle and a nephew. But the verse is translated differently in Christian Bibles, where uncovering the nakedness

of the uncle refers to sexual activity with the uncle's wife (see the *New Revised Standard Version* and the *New American Bible*).

8. Rabbinical understanding is that the prohibition against stealing in the Ten Commandments refers to kidnapping. This law bars all other stealing.

9. It is possible for a priest to be exempt from being circumcised according to Jewish law if his two older brothers died of circumcision. He may become a priest (Telushkin, *Biblical Literacy*, 551).

10. Law 356 is complicated. The reason no one can vow a firstborn animal to the LORD is because the firstborn already belongs to the LORD by well-established law (Exod 13:2; 22:29–30; Num 18:17). Rabbinical tradition sees this law as forbidding the exchange of one kind of sacrifice for another.

11. Deuteronomy 16:3 does not explicitly state that you shall not eat leaven past noon on the day of passover. This detail has been interjected here by rabbinical consensus.

12. Law 552 does not say that a marriage should take place before cohabitation, but this is a traditional rabbinical interpretation of the opening words of a casuistic law found in Deuteronomy 22:13–19.

13. The best Christian translations of Deuteronomy 23:18 restrict Israelite men and women from becoming *temple* prostitutes. Of course, the Deuteronomy laws are presented as being delivered to Israel centuries before there was a temple. The *Tanakh* uses this translation: "No Israelite woman shall be a cult prostitute, nor shall any Israelite man be a cult prostitute."

14. Jewish tradition understands Deuteronomy 31:19 as a command for every Jew to write a Torah scroll or contribute money to have a Torah scroll written (Telushkin, *Biblical Literacy*, 592).

7. The Decalogues of the Torah

1. According to Maimonides the first commandment is to believe that there is one God. Other medieval rabbis did not agree, saying that it is not rational to command someone to believe in God. Most Jewish scholars agree with Maimonides (Teluskin *Biblical Literacy*, 421–22).

2. Moshe Weinfeld, *Deuteronomy and the Deuteronomic School* (Oxford, Eng.: Oxford University Press, 1983), 248.

3. In Exodus the first time that the number ten is mentioned is in conjunction with the Ritual Decalogue of Exodus 34 (see Exod 34:28). The tablets of stone are mentioned for the first time in Exodus 24:12.

The tablets are mentioned again in Exodus 31:18 as an introduction to the story of the golden calf (Exod 32).

4. Another theological goal of the Aaronids (P) was to increase the population of the Judahite community of Babylon. As an integral part of the creation account the priestly command appears: "Be fruitful and multiply."

5. The phrase "outstretched arm" is a Deuteronomic expression.

6. See Childs, *Exodus*, 394.

7. Crusemann, *The Torah*, 352–55 (Crusemann cites Norbert Lohfink, *Unterschied*, 76).

8. Some translations read "the ten words."

9. Childs, *Exodus*, 601–9.

10. Scholars who attribute all or part of the Ritual Decalogue to J include, among others, Julius Wellhausen, Martin Noth, John Gray, Peter Ellis, Robert Coote, and Ronald Clements.

11. While it seems that verse 13 and other words and phrases of Exodus 34 are Deuteronomic, Frank Crusemann argues against this (see *Torah*, 117–20).

8. The Administration of Justice in Ancient Israel

1. Boecker, *Law and the Administration of Justice in the Old Testament*, 30–31. Boecker calls the Israelite legal assembly "the famous Hebrew legal assembly." This is strange, because the Israelites never called themselves Hebrews.

2. We can assume that certain people could not be part of a legal assembly: young people, women, slaves, and aliens.

3. Boecker, *Law and the Administration of Justice in the Old Testament*, 31. Boecker cites a German scholar, L. Kohler, who has estimated that Israel was made up of over forty distinct geographic districts. This fragmented topography would almost guarantee diversity of beliefs and practices. We are aware of many *local* traditions preserved for us in the Hebrew Bible.

4. There is a positive Midian tradition (Exod 19) and a negative Midian tradition (Num 31).

5. See, for example, 2 Samuel 18:1, where David selects commanders of thousands and commanders of hundreds.

6. Martin Noth, *Exodus: A Commentary* (Philadelphia: Westminster Press, 1962), 150.

7. In the Deuteronomic History, Jehoshaphat is not a champion of judicial procedure. Since Chronicles was written hundreds of years later, it is possible that the meaning of his name influenced the chronicler, removed so far from Jehoshaphat's reign. The name Jehoshaphat means "Yahweh establishes justice." Some scholars believe the Chronicles account is historical, however.

8. Many scholars believe that the Elijah cycle, of which the story of Naboth's vineyard is a part, was not included in the Josianic edition of the Deuteronomic History.

9. In Deuteronomy there are several places where a public speech is expected of certain participants. In addition to the recitation connected with this law (Deut 21:7–8), there is the creed in Deuteronomy 26:5–10 beginning with the words "A wandering Aramean was my ancestor," and later, after the paying of the tithe, the people are instructed to respond orally, beginning with the words "I have removed the sacred portion from the house, and I have given it to the Levites, the resident aliens, the orphans, and the widows" (Deut 26:13). Only in Deuteronomy are the people given an opportunity for a verbal response.

9. The Laws of the Ancient Near East

1. A collection of the laws of the ancient Near East has been published by Scholars Press as part of the Writings from the Ancient World Series (Martha T. Roth, ed., *Law Collections from Mesopotamia and Asia Minor* [Atlanta, Ga.: The Scholars Press, 1995]). The numbering of the laws in each collection and the abbreviations used in this chapter come from this volume.

2. The diorite pillar at the Louvre was excavated in 1901–2 at Susa, Iraq, where it had been taken as booty by an Elamite conqueror of Babylon. It is known that additional copies of the stela were erected in other Babylonian cities also.

3. There are a few scattered references in the laws of the ancient Near East that touch on religion. Blasphemy is mentioned without being defined, and witchcraft is a capital offense (MAL A47). Sacrifices are mentioned in a rare apodictic law (MAPD 47):

When the time for making sacrifices draws near, a palace woman who is menstruating shall not enter into the presence of the king.

In another rare apodictic law, a purification ritual is mentioned in Hittite Law 44b. A neo-Babylonian law also mentions an act of ritual purification (LNB 7).

4. Curiously, in the Hittite Laws there are four laws dealing with dogs (HL 87–90).

5. In addition to Roth, *Law Collections from Mesopotamia and Asia Minor,* a fully revised and expanded edition of *Old Testament Parallels: Law and Stories from the Ancient Near East,* ed. Victor H. Matthews and Don C. Benjamin (Mahwah, N.J.: Paulist Press, 1997) is available; this edition is also available on compact disk.

10. Oh, How I Love Your Law!

1. It is our belief that the Deuteronomic History, although it depended on multiple sources, was crafted as a theological history to promote the program summarized by the Deuteronomy Law Code (Deut 12—26) (see chapter 3, "The Law Code of Deuteronomy").

2. Martin Noth identified five separate traditional sources used in the creation of the Pentateuch. These five Pentateuchal traditions are (1) guidance out of Egypt, (2) guidance into the arable Land, (3) promise to the patriarchs, (4) guidance in the wilderness, and (5) revelation at Sinai (see Noth, *A History of Pentateuchal Tradition,* 46–62).

3. Just as in the Deuteronomic History, there are many doublets in the Pentateuch. Examples include two different reasons given for Jacob's fleeing to Paddan-aram, where he lived with his uncle Laban and married (Gen 27:41–45; 28:1–5). Another doublet involves the change of Jacob's name to Israel (Gen 32:27; 35:9–10).

4. Rainer Albertz, *A History of the Israelite Religion in the Old Testament Period,* vol. 2, *From the Exile to the Maccabees* (Louisville, Ky.: Westminster John Knox Press, 1994), 481.

5. See Chart 3c for eighteen ways in which the Deuteronomic Code is unique and differs from the Priestly Code and the Holiness Code.

6. See Roland Murphy, *New Jerome Biblical Commentary,* 4.

Appendix: Laws in the Book of Genesis

1. See chapter 6, "The Rabbinical Tradition of 613 Laws." In this tradition only three laws are counted as appearing in Genesis.

2. The word *covenant* also appears in Genesis 9:1–17 seven times, another chapter identified as a priestly source (see Ellis, *The Men and the Message of the Old Testament,* 58–59). When the priestly source uses the word *covenant,* the word does not imply the vassal

treaty structure that characterizes the Deuteronomic source (see Deut 4:1–40; 29—30).

3. Notice how the priestly wording suggests that sacrifices made in the open field are not sacrifices to the Lord. Verse 7 makes this specific: "so that they may no longer offer their sacrifices to goat-demons."

4. The three folk etiologies are the changing of Jacob's name to Israel (Gen 32:29); the name for Peniel (Gen 32:31); a food taboo forbidding the eating of the thigh muscle that is on the socket of the hip (Gen 32:32–33).

5. Rabbinical tradition counts this food taboo law as the third law of the Torah.

6. This is a J account that was inserted into the story of Joseph and his brothers. The reason for this placement is not clear.

For Further Reading

Ackerman, Susan. *Under Every Green Tree.* Atlanta, Ga.: Scholars Press, 1992.

Ahlstrom, Gosta W. *The History of Ancient Palestine.* Minneapolis, Minn.: Fortress Press, 1993.

Albertz, Rainer. *A History of Israelite Religion in the Old Testament Period.* Louisville, Ky.: Westminster John Knox Press, 1994.

Boecker, Hans Jochen. *Law and the Administration of Justice in the Old Testament.* Minneapolis, Minn.: Augsburg, 1980.

Childs, Brevard. *The Book of Exodus.* Philadelphia: Westminster Press, 1974.

Chill, Abraham. *The Mitzvot: The Commandments and Their Rationale.* New York: Bloch Publishing Company, 1974.

Clements, Ronald. *The Cambridge Bible Commentary, Exodus.* Cambridge, Eng.: University Press, 1972.

Coote, Robert and Mary. *Power, Politics and the Making of the Bible.* Minneapolis, Minn.: Fortress Press, 1994.

Crusemann, Frank. *The Torah: Theology and Social History of Old Testament Law.* Minneapolis, Minn.: Fortress Press, 1996.

Doorly, William J. *Obsession with Justice, The Story of the Deuteronomists.* Mahwah, N.J.: Paulist Press, 1994.

———. *The Religion of Israel.* Mahwah, N.J.: Paulist Press, 1997.

Dozeman, Thomas. *God on the Mountain.* Atlanta, Ga.: Scholars Press, 1989.

Ellis, Peter F. *The Men and the Message of the Old Testament.* Collegeville, Minn.: Liturgical Press, 1963.

Freidman, Richard Elliott. *The Exile and Biblical Narrative.* Chico, Calif.: Scholars Press, 1981.

Gottwald, Norman K. *The Hebrew Bible: A Socio-Literary Introduction.* Philadelphia: Fortress Press, 1985.

Hopkins, David. *The Highlands of Canaan: Agriculture in the Early Iron Age.* Sheffield: JSOT Press, 1985.

Kahan, Rabbi A. Y. *The Taryag Mitzvos.* Brooklyn, N.Y.: Keser Torah Publications, 1987.

Matthews, Victor H., and Don C. Benjamin. *Old Testament Parallels.* Mahwah, N.J.: Paulist Press, 1997.

Mayes, A. D. H. *The New Century Bible Commentary, Deuteronomy.* Grand Rapids, Mich.: Eerdmans, 1991.

Milgrom, Jacob. *Leviticus 1—16,* vol. 3 of the Anchor Bible. New York: Doubleday, 1991.

Murphy, Roland E. *Responses to 101 Questions on the Biblical Torah.* Mahwah, N.J.: Paulist Press, 1996.

Noth, Martin. *Exodus: A Commentary.* Philadelphia: Westminster Press, 1962.

Patrick, Dale, ed. *Thinking Biblical Law, Semeia* 45. Atlanta, Ga.: Scholars Press, 1989.

Redford, Donald B. *Egypt, Canaan, Israel in Ancient Times.* Princeton, N.J.: Princeton University Press, 1992.

Roth, Martha T., ed. *Law Collection from Mesopotamia and Asia Minor.* Atlanta, Ga.: Scholars Press, 1995.

Sanders, James A. *Torah and Canon.* Philadelphia: Fortress Press, 1972.

Soggin, J. Alberto. *Introduction to the Old Testament.* Philadelphia: Westminster Press, 1976.

Telushkin, Joseph, *Biblical Literacy.* New York: William Morrow and Company, 1997.

Von Rad, Gerhard. *Deuteronomy.* 4th ed. Philadelphia: Westminster Press, 1975.

Weinfeld, Moshe. *Deuteronomy and the Deuteronomic School.* Oxford, Eng.: Oxford University Press, 1983.

An Index to the Laws of the Torah

(Sorted by key words)

The locations of the laws in the index are identified by the following letter codes:

The Covenant Code/Book of the Covenant	BC
The Deuteronomic Code	DC
The Book of Genesis	GN
The Holiness Code	HC
The Priestly Code	PC
Ten Commandments/Ethical Decalogue	TC
Ritual Decalogue	RD
Deuteronomy Before and After the Deuteronomic Code	DT

Death makes all under the same roof to be unclean	Num 19:14–15	PC
Debts, Remission of every seven years	Deut 15:1–6	DC
Decision of central judges, Carry out diligently	Deut 17:10–11	DC
Defect, You shall not sacrifice an animal with a	Deut 17:1	DC
Defile, Do not…yourselves	Lev 18:24–30	HC
Defraud your neighbor, You shall not	Lev 19:13	HC
Dependents shall not become slaves	Lev 25:39	HC
Destroy shrines of other gods in the land	Deut 12:2	DC
Dies of itself, Do not eat anything that	Deut 14:21	DC
Dispossessed people, Do not imitate their rites	Deut 12:29–32	DC
Divorced wife, A husband cannot remarry his	Deut 24:1–4	DC
Divorced woman, Priests shall not marry a	Lev 21:7	HC
Donations, Sacred to be consumed at chosen place	Deut 12:26	DC
Donations, The unclean may not eat sacred	Lev 22:1–7	HC
Donkey and an ox together, Do not plow with	Deut 22:10	DC
Donkey must be redeemed, Firstborn	Exod 13:13	PC
Donkey must be redeemed with a sheep, Firstborn	Exod 13:13	PC
Donkey must be redeemed with a sheep, Firstborn	Exod 34:20	RD
Donkey of an enemy found overburdened	Exod 23:5	BC
Donkey or ox if fallen, neighbor must assist	Deut 22:4	DC
Doorposts of your house, Write the laws on the	Deut 6:9	DT
Dough set aside as an offering (hallah)	Num 15:17–21	PC
Eat your fill, Bless Yahweh when you	Deut 8:10	DT
Edomite, Do not abhor. They are your kin.	Deut 23:7	DC
Egypt, Tell your son of your liberation from	Exod 13:8	PC
Egypt, You shall not live as its inhabitants do	Lev 18:3	HC
Egyptian, Do not abhor. You dwelt in their land	Deut 23:7	DC
Elevation offering as part of festival of weeks	Lev 23:17–20	HC
Empty-handed, Do not send a male slave out	Deut 15:13	DC
Empty-handed, No one shall appear before me	Exod 34:20	RD
Enemy army, Do not be fearful before a large	Deut 20:1–4	DC
Exchanging sacrifice types is forbidden	Lev 27:26	PC
Exchanging animals in an offering forbidden	Lev 27:10	PC
Eye for eye, tooth for tooth	Lev 24:19, 21	HC
Eye for eye, tooth for tooth, hand for hand…	Deut 19:21	DC

Firstborn of your male livestock shall be redeemed	Exod 34:19	RD
Firstborn of your sons shall be redeemed	Exod 34:20	RD
Firstborn son, Rights of	Deut 21:15–17	DC
Firstling: Eat at the LORD's chosen place	Deut 15:20	DC
Firstling, If it has a defect do not sacrifice	Deut 15:21–22	DC
Firstling male born of flock to be consecrated	Deut 15:19	DC
Flesh touching an unclean thing not to be eaten	Lev 7:19	PC
Flogging to be done in the presence of a judge	Deut 25:1–3	DC
Flour as a substitute offering for turtledoves	Lev 5:11–13	PC
Flour, A sin offering of choice	Lev 5:11–13	PC
Follow other gods, Do not	Deut 6:14	DT
Food at a profit, Do not provide…for kin	Lev 25:37	HC
Forehead, Fix the laws as an emblem on your	Deut 6:8	DT
Foreigner may not eat of the passover	Exod 12:43	PC
Forget not Yahweh when you have eaten your fill	Deut 6:10–12	DT
Fourteenth day of Nisan kill lamb at twilight	Exod 12:6	PC
Framework of the tabernacle, Details of the	Exod 26:15–30	PC
Frankincense, A sin offering of flour without	Lev 5:11	PC
Fraud, When property is obtained by theft or	Lev 6:1–7	PC
Freewill offering must be perfect	Lev 22:21–25	HC
Freewill or votive offering, When sacrifice is	Lev 7:16–18	PC
Fringes required on the corners of garments	Num 15:37–41	PC
Fruit, Eat the fourth year in Jerusalem	Lev 19:23	HC
Fruit not to be eaten first three years from tree	Lev 19:23	HC
Fruitful and multiply, Be	Gen 1:28	GN
Gashes in their flesh, Priests shall not make	Lev 21:5	HC
Gashes in your flesh for the dead forbidden	Lev 19:28	HC
Genitals, A man with injured…restricted	Deut 23:1–2	DC
Genitals, When a wife grabs when two men fight	Deut 25:11–12	DC
Goat-demons, Sacrifices to…forbidden	Lev 17:7	HC
Gods before me, You shall have no other	Exod 20:3	TC
Gods before me, You shall have no other	Deut 5:7	TC
Gold altar, There will be no offerings on the	Exod 30:9	PC
Grain offering to be divided among priests	Lev 7:8–10	PC
Grapes, When you gather them do not glean all	Deut 24:21	DC
Grapes, When you harvest do not be thorough	Deut 24:21	DC
Grapes, You may pick and eat from your neighbor	Deut 23:24	DC

Idols: Carved images or pillars are forbidden	Lev 26:1	HC
Idols of anything on land or sea are forbidden	Exod 20:4	TC
Idols of anything on land or sea are forbidden	Deut 5:8	TC
Idols, You shall not bow down to or worship	Exod 20:5	TC
Idols, You shall not bow down to or worship	Deut 5:9	TC
Idols, You shall not make cast	Exod 34:17	RD
Images and idols, Do not turn to	Lev 19:4	HC
Images, Do not covet gold or silver of their	Deut 7:25	DT
Images of gold and silver forbidden	Exod 20:23	BC
Images of their gods you shall burn with fire	Deut 7:25	DT
Incense, Altar of	Exod 30:10	PC
Incense, Every morning Aaron shall burn	Exod 30:7	PC
Incense, Restrictions on replicating temple	Exod 30:37	PC
Ingathering, Festival of	Exod 23:16b	BC
Ingathering, Observe at the turn of the year	Exod 34:22	RD
Inheritance laws when a man dies	Num 27:8–11	PC
Inheritance shall not transfer to another tribe	Num 36:7, 9	PC
Inheritance, Woman with…will marry within tribe	Num 36:8	PC
Innocent blood, Purging the guilt of	Deut 21:3–9	DC
Insects with four legs that may be eaten	Lev 11:20–23	PC
Insects with wings are forbidden food	Deut 14:19	DC
Interest, Dependent kin shall not pay in advance	Lev 25:35–38	HC
Interest, Do not charge an Israelite	Deut 23:19	DC
Interest, You may charge to foreigners	Deut 23:20	DC
Intermarry with the dislodged nations, Do not	Deut 7:3	DT
Jealousy, Law in cases of	Num 5:11–31	PC
Jubilee: Houses in open country shall be released	Lev 25:31	HC
Jubilee year observed every fiftieth year	Lev 25:8–12	HC
Jubilee year, Sale price of property adjusted for	Lev 25:13–17	HC
Judgment, You shall not render unjust	Lev 19:15	HC
Judges, Guidelines for rendering decisions	Deut 16:19–20	DC
Judges, You shall appoint throughout your tribes	Deut 16:18	DC
Judicial decision, Any who refuses to carry out	Deut 17:12	DC
Justice due to your poor in their lawsuits	Exod 23:6	BC
Kid not to be boiled in its mother's milk	Exod 23:19b	BC
Kid not to be boiled in its mother's milk	Exod 34:26b	RD
Kid not to be boiled in its mother's milk	Deut 14:21b	DC

Levites, Do not neglect resident	Deut 12:19	DC
Levites, Do not neglect them	Deut 14:27	DC
Levites may come to central shrine and minister	Deut 18:6–7	DC
Levites, Pasture lands provided for	Num 35:2–5	PC
Levites, Responsibilities differ from Aaronids	Num 18:2–7	PC
Levites shall have equal portions	Deut 18:8	DC
Levites to have no allotment among Israelites	Num 18:23	PC
Levites to receive a tithe of Israel's offerings	Num 18:24	PC
Levites, Towns for Levites to live in	Num 35:2–8	PC
Levitical priests shall have no land inheritance	Deut 18:1–2	DC
Lie to one another, You shall not	Lev 19:11	HC
Lost donkey or garment, Obligations if found	Deut 22:3	DC
Love the alien as yourself	Lev 19:34	HC
Love the stranger, You shall	Deut 10:19	DT
Love Yahweh with all your heart, You shall	Deut 6:5	DT
Love Yahweh your God and keep his charge	Deut 11:1	DT
Love Yahweh your God and walk in his ways	Deut 10:12	DT
Love Yahweh your God with all your heart	Deut 13:3	DC
Love your neighbor as yourself	Lev 19:18	HC
Maims, One who…shall receive the same	Lev 24:19, 21	HC
Male homosexual behavior is forbidden	Lev 18:22	HC
Man shall not lie with a man as with a woman	Lev 20:13	HC
Materials in a garment must not be mixed	Lev 19:19	HC
Meal offering with oil and frankincense	Lev 2:1–3	PC
Measurements, You shall not cheat in	Lev 19:35	HC
Measures, You shall not have two kinds	Deut 25:13–16	DC
Meat, Consumption of and profane slaughter	Deut 12:20–22	DC
Meat, Do not eat abhorrent or forbidden	Deut 14:3–8	DC
Meat mangled by beasts in the field	Exod 22:31	BC
Medium and wizard shall be put to death	Lev 20:27	HC
Mediums and wizards, Consulting them is forbidden	Lev 20:6	HC
Mediums and wizards you shall not seek out	Lev 19:31	HC
Menstruating woman, Do not approach	Lev 18:19	HC
Menstruating woman, Sex with her is forbidden	Lev 20:18	HC
Mill or millstone not to be taken in pledge	Deut 24:6	DC
Moabite, barred from the assembly of the LORD	Deut 23:3	DC
Molech must be stoned, Persons who offer to	Lev 20:1–5	HC
Money or goods kept for safekeeping	Exod 22:7–8	BC
Money, Exchanging your sacrifice for	Deut 14:25	DT
Month, Offerings required at the start of	Num 28:11–15	PC

Neighbor's wife is forbidden, Adultery with	Lev 20:10	HC
Newborn animal remains with its mother seven days	Lev 22:26	HC
Newly married man entitled to military-free year	Deut 24:5	DC
Nocturnal emission of a man who is encamped	Deut 23:10–11	DC
Oath, When a person utters a rash	Lev 5:4	PC
Offerings from your fullness, no delay	Exod 22:29	BC
Oil: Special anointing…for the high priests	Exod 30:32	PC
Oil to anoint priests, Requirements for	Exod 30:25–30	PC
Olive trees, Do not strip them completely	Deut 24:20	DC
One law for both alien and citizen	Lev 24:22	HC
Open land around Levite cities cannot be sold	Lev 25:34	HC
Ordinances, You shall observe my	Lev 18:4	HC
Other gods, Worshipers of to be stoned	Deut 17:2–5	DC
Ownership of property when disputed	Exod 22:9	BC
Ox and a donkey together, Do not plow with	Deut 22:10	DC
Ox: Do not muzzle when it treads out the grain	Deut 25:4	DC
Ox gores a boy or a girl, When an	Exod 21:31	BC
Ox gores a male or female slave, When an	Exod 21:32	BC
Ox gores a man or woman, When an	Exod 21:28	BC
Ox hurts an ox of another	Exod 21:35–36	BC
Ox or donkey of your enemy going astray	Exod 23:4	BC
Ox or a sheep, When someone steals an	Exod 22:1, 4	BC
Parapet required on roof of a new house	Deut 22:8	DC
Parents: Any who curse them shall be put to death	Lev 20:8	HC
Parents shall not be punished for child's crimes	Deut 24:16	DC
Partial in judging, You shall not be	Deut 1:17	DT
Paschal lamb, No bone shall be broken of the	Exod 12:46	PC
Paschal lamb to be left till dawn, No portion of	Exod 12:10	PC
Paschal lamb to be eaten at place of slaughter	Exod 12:46	PC
Paschal lamb to be eaten with bitter herbs	Exod 12:8	PC
Paschal lamb to be eaten with unleavened bread	Exod 12:8	PC
Paschal lamb to be roasted, not boiled	Exod 12:9	PC
Paschal lamb to be slaughtered at twilight	Exod 12:6	PC
Passover and festival of unleavened bread	Lev 23:5–8	HC
Passover, Foreigner may not eat of the	Exod 12:43	PC
Passover, Hired servant may not eat of the	Exod 12:45	PC
Passover, How to observe correctly	Deut 16:1–8	DC
Passover, If ignored for no good reason	Num 9:13	PC

Ransom: Life of a murderer cannot be ransomed	Num 35:31	PC
Raped, A betrothed virgin in the city	Deut 22:23–24	DC
Raped in the country an engaged woman goes free	Deut 22:25–27	DC
Raped woman must cry out	Deut 22:23–24	DC
Read this law to all Israel every seven years	Deut 31:10	DT
Red heifer law	Num 19:2–8	PC
Redemption for kin who belong to resident alien	Lev 25:47–55	HC
Refuge: Cities of…for unintentional killers	Num 35:9–15	PC
Refuge, Selecting three more cities if necessary	Deut 19:8–9	DC
Refuge: Slayer remains in…until high priest dies	Num 35:25	PC
Refuge, When an intentional murderer flees to city	Deut 19:11–13	DC
Refuge, When to increase cities of	Deut 19:8–10	DC
Refuge, You shall establish three cities of	Deut 19:1–7	DC
Remission of debts is not required for foreigner	Deut 15:3	DC
Resident aliens may become slaves	Lev 25:45	HC
Sabbath day observance	Exod 23:12–13	BC
Sabbath day: Observe it and keep it holy	Deut 5:12–15	TC
Sabbath day of complete rest to be observed	Lev 23:3	HC
Sabbath day offerings, Required	Num 28:9–10	PC
Sabbath day: You shall keep it holy	Exod 20:8–11	TC
Sabbath, Kindle no fire on the	Exod 35:37	PC
Sabbath, Let no man leave his location on the	Exod 16:29	PC
Sabbath year for your fields	Exod 23:10–11	BC
Sabbath year of rest for the land required	Lev 25:1–7	HC
Sabbaths, You shall keep my	Lev 19:3	HC
Sabbaths, You shall keep my	Lev 19:30	HC
Sabbaths, You shall reverence my	Lev 26:2	HC
Sacred donations, A lay person shall not eat	Lev 22:10	HC
Sacred donations belong to the priests	Num 5:9–10	PC
Sacred donations, Limitations described	Lev 22:10–16	HC
Sacred donations, servant of priest shall not	Lev 22:10	HC
Sacred donations, The unclean may not eat	Lev 22:1–7	HC
Sacred donations, Those born in priest's house	Lev 22:11	HC
Sacred pole, You shall not plant next to altar	Deut 16:21	DC
Sacrifice of well-being must be done correctly	Lev 19:5	HC
Sacrifice of well-being to be eaten by second day	Lev 19:6–8	HC
Sacrifice only at the LORD's chosen place	Deut 12:13–14	DC